A Is for ADAM

Biblical Baby Names

by Lorilee Craker • art by Mona Daly

WATERBROOK
PRESS

"A" Is for Adam
Published by WaterBrook Press
5446 North Academy Boulevard, Suite 200
Colorado Springs, Colorado 80918
A division of Random House, Inc.

ISBN 1-57856-324-0

Printed in the United States of America

2000—First Edition

10 9 8 7 6 5 4 3 2 1

FOR JONAH ABRAM REIMER CRAKER:

We've never been the same since you joined us, Jo Jo.
You really are the boy of our dreams.
May you, like the ancient prophet with your name,
use your strong will to serve God.
Even if he sends you to your idea of Nineveh,
always remember there is a perfect reason for it.

(Hint: Just go the first time!)

Introduction

I guess my penchant for biblical nomenclature started before I was even born. I grew up in the Canadian prairies, descended from a long line of Abrahams on one side and Isaacs on the other. No, I'm not Jewish; I'm Mennonite, a faith tradition that has long made excellent use of spiritual name-sakes from the Bible. It cracks me up that Jacob is the number two most popular boys' name—every Mennonite worth his or her salt has at least one Uncle Jake in the family tree. To me, the name conjures up an old Mennonite Opa type, not a freckle-faced hockey player who can barely stand up in his skates! But that's the thing about Bible names: They are so timeless, so durable, so perennially appealing, it is possible to have an ancient great-uncle and an adorable nephew both dubbed Jacob by their adoring parents. And I do!

Many of my peers, today's parents in their twenties and thirties, want their babys' names to say a lot. They want to give their precious progeny a handle that will stand them in good stead for the rest of their lives. But more than a sturdy, it-will-do kind of name, young couples of faith want a name that will reflect their bedrock beliefs, especially in a pluralistic culture like ours.

In this little book, I have chosen the most beautiful, interesting, and viable choices from the Good Book, not only God's inspired revelation, but also a fabulous source of fresh, gorgeous—and spiritually meaningful—names. I have left out about three thousand monikers, but were you guys really considering Hephzibah anyway? I didn't think so. There's something here for everyone: classic aficionados, trendy types, quirky folks. And if a name appeals to you, the profile will include just about every detail, nuance, and trivia particle associated with it. After all, would you buy a new car simply by picking it off a dictionary listing of ten thousand automobiles? Of course not. So why wouldn't you want the entire scoop on the social identification tag you are about to bestow on a helpless infant, the name your darling child will be using for the next eighty years? There's even a magazine-type quiz for the ladies (and men who are roped into participating) to help you narrow down your list.

I do have one disclaimer: Even though loads of research went into these name paragraphs, ultimately, they reflect my opinion. You won't agree with every profile, but my hope is that I have given you some great ideas to start you on your way. Your baby is so special and peerless and one of a kind! He or she deserves the best name you can come up with.

—Lorilee Craker

Abigail

Could there be a more charming, appealing name than Abigail? As the beautiful wife of King David, Abigail lived up to a name that bespeaks feminine softness and an underlying strength of character. When Nabal, her selfish, narrow-minded first husband, refused to take care of David's servants, despite the latter's generosity, Abigail took matters into her own hands, averting disaster and saving the day. David was so impressed he married her when Nabal died. Parents who choose this jewel for their daughter are probably attracted to antiques, classic books, and all things old-fashioned yet enduring. Abigail means "fountain of joy" or "father's joy" in Hebrew, making it an ideal choice for a dad-to-be who plans to cherish his little girl. As a bonus, Abby is everything a nickname should be: adorable for a child without being silly for an adult.

Abra

Abra (AH-brah), a diminutive and feminization of Abraham, has a purely beautiful, ethereal sound, is imaginative and unique, and is even infused with a literary essence thanks to John Steinbeck's capricious character in *East of Eden*. When all of Abra's positives are considered, it seems like the perfect designation for a baby girl. But there is one caveat: Even though its softness would suit a sensitive little girl, would such a tender child be able to withstand teasing for having "bra" in her name? Savvy parents-to-be would do well to consider possible ways their child's name could be maligned by wee wise guys. But if you decide you and your little Abra can handle this—after all, such teasing is sure to be short-lived—people will likely think of your daughter as being creative and arty before they even meet her. Such is the innovative power this name carries.

The Top Fifty Girls' Names

1. Emily
2. Hannah*
3. Samantha
4. Ashley
5. Sarah*
6. Alexis
7. Taylor
8. Jessica
9. Madison
10. Elizabeth*
11. Alyssa
12. Megan
13. Kayla
14. Lauren
15. Rachel*
16. Victoria
17. Brianna
18. Amanda
19. Abigail*
20. Jennifer
21. Emma
22. Olivia
23. Morgan
24. Nicole
25. Brittany
26. Jasmine
27. Stephanie
28. Alexandra
29. Sydney
30. Rebecca*
31. Julia*
32. Anna*
33. Katherine
34. Allison
35. Amber
36. Kaitlyn
37. Hayley
38. Destiny
39. Courtney
40. Danielle
41. Natalie
42. Jordan*
43. Maria
44. Brooke
45. Savannah
46. Jasmine
47. Gabrielle
48. Sara*
49. Madeline
50. Shelby

*Profiles found elsewhere in "A" Is for Adam

Acacia

Attention tree huggers: You won't find Acacia (ah-KAY-shuh) in many baby-name books. This feminine moniker is as fine and rare as the acacia tree from which the Israelites crafted the ark and the tabernacle. In Exodus 25, God told his people through Moses to offer precious materials to him such as gold, silver, fine linens, and acacia wood, a high-quality brown and apricot-colored hardwood that was and still is excellent for making furniture. This lyrical name is commonly used in Greece and means "resurrection tree." With highly usable nicknames such as Casia (KAY-shuh) or even Casey, Acacia is perfect if you are looking for an edgy name with deep, spiritual symbolism. Botanists and other forms of nature lovers as well as wood craftsmen of all kinds may find that Acacia dovetails perfectly with their vocation or hobby.

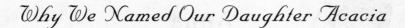

Why We Named Our Daughter Acacia

We adopted our brown-eyed, olive-skinned, God-chosen daughter eleven years ago. When she came to our home at three months old, her foster mother already had chosen a name for her, but we decided to name her ourselves, a privilege of parenthood.

We chose the name Acacia, knowing that acacia wood was used to build the ark of the covenant. *Covenant* is a strong word. For us it evokes a sense of God's gracious, tenacious promises. Acacia was our promise child. We also learned that the acacia tree, which grows in African semiarid climates, among other places, stays green even when the rest of the vegetation dries up, providing shade for animals and people.

Since our Acacia is part African American, we wanted her name to reflect her heritage. Now, she loves to spend time with babies, protecting them, holding them close in her arms, shielding them from danger. By modeling for little ones the covenant God who loves children, our Acacia is living up to her name quite beautifully!

—Dave and Melanie Beelen

Anna

Anna is what baby-name book writer Joal Ryan calls a *Little House on the Prairie* name. Indeed Anna brings to mind a pioneer who left her homeland to toil by day under the hot sun and sleep at night under a sod roof. Though she is climbing the popularity charts, this stylish classic has the backbone to withstand the trendy tempests of Ashley and Aubrey—there is nothing froufrou about Anna! The biblical bearer of the name, which means "full of grace, fortunate," was called a prophetess, indicating that she was exceptionally close to God: "She never left the temple but worshiped night and day, fasting and praying" (Luke 2:37). Anna has been bestowed on countless literary heroines, including Tolstoy's *Anna Karenina*. Refined, intelligent, and imbued with an unmistakable European charm, Anna is the ideal choice for those who want to honor relatives from the old country, or those who simply want a strong name for their baby.

Place Names from the Bible

- Alexandria
- Berea
- Bethany*
- Cana/Canaan
- Carmel
- Eden*
- Israel
- Janoah
- Jericho
- Jordan*
- Marah*
- Moriah
- Shiloh*
- Zion*

*Profiles found elsewhere in "A" Is for Adam

Ariel

Let's get the mermaid out of the way first. Yes, perhaps a dozen children will connect your little Ariel with the cartoon character from Disney's animated musical. Is that so bad? No, especially considering Ariel the mermaid is a sweet, positive character (not, for example, Cruella deVille!). Beyond the movie, Ariel has a long and illustrious history in literature from *The Tempest* to Sylvia Plath's poem *Ariel*. This Hebrew name, well used for boys and girls in modern-day Israel, was even conferred on the moon that orbits the planet Uranus, which may explain its rather unearthly, ethereal image. There is nothing wispy, though, about Ariel's meaning, "lioness of God," or its origin in Scripture as a leader who served under Ezra (Ezra 8:16). Also, Ariel is a poetic name for the city of Jerusalem. (Featuring the same prefix, Arabella is picking up steam among the elite. Listen for the *air* sound to travel far.)

Why We Named Our Daughter Arielle

While anticipating the birth of our second child, my husband and I were tossing around a variety of girl names. Allison...maybe. Caitlyn...already taken by a cousin. Nicole...Hmm...I liked the sound of it, but something wasn't right. We sat down one night surrounded by eight baby-name books from a local library and started saying names. We found our favorite in the *A*'s: Arielle.

The name Arielle incorporates two very important parts of our life—the Bible and fine literature: Ariel is an alternative name for Jerusalem and also a character in the Shakespeare play *The Tempest*. So we named our new daughter Arielle only to have one of our visitors at the hospital say with obvious shock, "I cannot believe that you named your child after a Disney character!" Unbeknownst to us, *The Little Mermaid* was the new Disney hit and Ariel the name of the feisty lead character. True to her cartoon name-sake, Arielle is a strong swimmer—even without a fish tail.

—*Dwight and Tammy Baker*

Bethany

Bethany, a village two miles east of Jerusalem near the road to Jericho, was very special to Jesus. A family he loved dearly—sisters Mary and Martha and their brother, Lazarus—lived there. He often stayed with them, and the bond they shared was significant. Also three pivotal events in Jesus' life took place in Bethany: He raised his friend Lazarus from the dead (John 11:38-44); his feet were anointed by Mary with expensive perfume, worth a year's wages (John 12:1-11); and he bid farewell to his earthly ministry and to his disciples, blessing them and ascending into heaven (Luke 24:50-51). Choosing Bethany (a name that means "worships God") would honor this significant village in Jesus' life; plus your daughter would have a graceful, quaint, and still-fresh Bible name with abundant spiritual application. Bonus: Bethany is stronger, deeper, and far less dated than Brittany, the similar sounding but inferior princess label belonging to a good 10 percent of the class of 2010.

Chloe

Chloe simply blooms with possibility and promise, energy and well-being. This Greek name, which means "verdant, fresh young blossom," is a dynamic, upscale choice that has it all over such wilting competitors as Caitlin and Courtney. This winning designation also boasts an interesting history: Seventeenth-century Puritans, who refused to dub their daughters with any Catholic or Anglican saints' names, scoured the New Testament for new options and unearthed a passing reference to a certain Chloe in 1 Corinthians 1:11. Soon Puritan play groups had wee Chloes running around, no doubt the life of the party amongst their playmates Prudence and Resolved! In literature Chloe was the girl who fell in love with Daphnis in the third-century, Greek pastoral, prose romance, fittingly titled *Daphnis and Chloe*. A modern, vibrant, and exceptionally pretty choice.

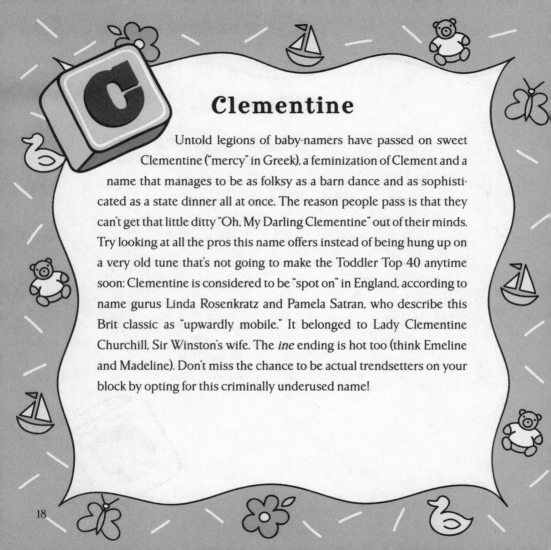

Clementine

Untold legions of baby-namers have passed on sweet Clementine ("mercy" in Greek), a feminization of Clement and a name that manages to be as folksy as a barn dance and as sophisticated as a state dinner all at once. The reason people pass is that they can't get that little ditty "Oh, My Darling Clementine" out of their minds. Try looking at all the pros this name offers instead of being hung up on a very old tune that's not going to make the Toddler Top 40 anytime soon: Clementine is considered to be "spot on" in England, according to name gurus Linda Rosenkratz and Pamela Satran, who describe this Brit classic as "upwardly mobile." It belonged to Lady Clementine Churchill, Sir Winston's wife. The *ine* ending is hot too (think Emeline and Madeline). Don't miss the chance to be actual trendsetters on your block by opting for this criminally underused name!

Damaris

An obscure Bible name, Damaris means "a gentle woman" in Greek. Indeed the very sound of the name evokes serenity, compassion, and composure. In the pagan city of Athens, Paul preached a rousing apologetic sermon comparing stone idols with the risen Savior, and Damaris was singled out as the one woman who professed faith in Christ that day (Acts 17:34). The best-selling novel *A Woman Named Damaris* by Janette Oke has raised the profile of this name.

Deborah

Deborah is a biblical role model possessing great valor, sound judgment, and a heart after God. The fifth Judge in Israel and a prophetess, Deborah commanded the respect of the entire nation, even Barak, Israel's military general, who wouldn't go into battle against the Canaanites without her! "Very well," Deborah said, "I will go with you. But because of the way you are going about this, the honor will not be yours, for the Lord will hand Sisera over to a woman" (Judges 4:9). Take that, Barak! This alias burned up the baby-name charts from the fifties through the midseventies, but is starting to sound distinctive again after a cooling-off period of twenty-five years. Like Elizabeth, however, Deborah must be used in its fullest form. Debbie was nice while it lasted, but don't use it unless you want to name your other children Kelly, Kenny, and Jodi.

Dinah

If you can keep from humming "Someone's in the Kitchen with Dinah" every time you and your daughter are baking cookies, this vivid Hebrew handle is cool, hip, jazzy—and positively ripe for the picking as a girl's name. (The "jazzy" part is probably due to jazz great Dinah Washington.) Dinah is a best-kept secret in the realm of baby naming. It's in no danger of becoming trendy (though for over two centuries—seventeenth through the nineteenth—it was a very hot choice), and it offers the whole package: pretty, strong sounding, with a fabulous meaning ("justified") and even the *ah* ending so appealing to modern young couples. Choosing Dinah will set your daughter apart from the crowd without drawing undue attention to her unusual name. The biblical Dinah was the only recorded daughter among Jacob's many children (Genesis 34:1). Note of caution: Be aware that the account of Dinah in Genesis 34 tells a disturbing tale of a woman violated. She was, as far as we know, a person who was unfairly victimized, but unfortunately, Scripture tells us no more about Dinah's life.

Drusilla

People will probably think you made up Drusilla until you tell them your baby girl had a biblical forerunner: The Jewish wife of Felix, Drusilla listened to Paul's address on faith (Acts 24:24). This three-syllable powerhouse packs an attitude, so it's no wonder it means "the strong one." Those turbo baby-namers, the Puritans, made good use of Drusilla, never dreaming that someday this name would be revived again by the writers of *The Young and the Restless*, who dubbed a feisty character thus. Bonus: Depending on how you view it, Drusilla is either the long form of the ultrahot, gender-neutral Drew, or Drew is the cute, tomboyish nickname of Drusilla. (You can call your daughter Drew from the delivery room onward, but she still has a longer, formal name to fall back on for, say, her law school applications.)

Eden

This lovely biblical place name takes us back to the garden paradise where our story as humans started. In Eden anything and everything was possible, and beauty and freedom abounded in a way never since experienced by mortals (Genesis 2:8–3:24). Slightly sudsy around the edges (it has been used in a soap opera), Eden gives off a glamorous, larger-than-life aura. Still baby-name experts are unanimous in their glowing recommendations: "As natural and unadorned as a fig leaf wardrobe," raves Ryan. Rosenkratz and Satran agree. Place names are hot, and Eden "strikes an appealing balance between the big country Dakotas and Montanas and the ultraexotic Asias and Kenyas." Bonus: Don't be surprised if your own Eden cultivates an early interest in gardening! Literary reference: John Steinbeck's novel *East of Eden*.

Eliya / Elisha

Here are two wonderfully differentiated choices that not only maximize the boy-names-for-girls trend, they also share ultrapleasing sounds with some overdone girls' names. Eliya (El-EE-yah), the feminine of Elijah, is aurally musical and ladylike without being too ruffles-and-lace. Parents who are attracted to the prevalent Elise or Alyssa will find a fresher, more distinctive choice in this Hebrew name meaning "the Lord is my God." Elisha (El-LIGH-shah) was the name of Elijah's protégé who parted the Jordan River. (Both prophets' stories unfold in 1 and 2 Kings.) His name sounds much more like hers to the modern ear and even shares a few commonalities with chart-buster Ashley. It goes without saying that Elisha would be infinitely stronger and more interesting. Ellie is the appealing nickname in both cases.

Elizabeth

Fully one-quarter of Renaissance parents coronated their daughters with the royal name Elizabeth, no doubt to honor their fierce queen, Elizabeth I. (Of course the current British monarch, a wise and gracious ruler, is also her namesake.) This perennial favorite is still locked into position on the top twenty, currently at number ten. Why? Elegance, regal bearing, history, and sheer beauty all play a part. The Greek form of the Hebrew *Elisheva* or *Elisheba*, Elizabeth means "consecrated to God." The biblical Elizabeth became pregnant late in life with a son who would grow up to be John the Baptist. The deeply spiritual woman rejoiced when her also-pregnant cousin Mary visited her, realizing instantly that Mary's unborn child was the Messiah. If you love this name beyond all reasoning—and why shouldn't you?—go ahead and use it, but be warned that many, many other parents will do likewise. For twenty-first-century babies, Lizzie, Ellie, and Libby rise above Elizabeth's countless other short forms.

Esther

Esther is one of the truly magnificent heroines in the Bible. Because the King of Persia chose her as his queen based on her looks, she presumably was a beauty of supermodel standards. But Esther was much more than a pretty face. Together with her cousin, Mordecai, she devised a plan to save her people from the genocidal plot being hatched by the egomaniac Haman. Her amazing resourcefulness, savvy, tact, and courage saved the Jews from certain annihilation, and to this day Jews celebrate her story on the holiday of Purim. A Persian name meaning "star" (most likely referring to the planet Venus), Esther sounds a like a woman with a high IQ and chutzpah to spare. After seventy-five years in the cedar chest of names, Esther should be dusted off and used with pride for the gutsy girls of the new millennium.

Why We Named Our Daughter Esther

We have sought the Lord in the naming of each of our children (five in all), and the Lord has amazed us with each answer to our prayers. Our fourth child was given the name Esther because of the story of Esther in the Bible. At two years old our Esther already loves to pray. With help she prays for relatives and neighbors that need salvation. She is also strong-willed, a quality necessary in a strong leader. We believe the Lord is preparing Esther "for such a time as this" (Esther 4:14) and has a special plan for her life. As parents we pray that the Lord would develop her character and that she will, like the biblical character of Esther, be given the courage for the work the Lord has prepared in advance for her to do.

—*Dan and Dawn Uitvlugt*

Pet Names from the Bible

Bird
Gabriel
Zipporah

Bullfrog
Jeremiah

Cat
Delilah
Eunice
Felix
Ichabod
Jezebel
Lazarus
Lilith
Linus
Methuselah
Persis
Phineas
Shadrach

Solomon
Tabitha
Tobias
Zaza

Chicken
Oved

Cow
Milcah

Dog
Abednego
Abner
Barcas
Beno
Crispus
Ebenezer
Festus
Goliath (for Great
   Dane /Chihuahua)

Gomer
Hermon
Hulda ("to dig")
Jehoshaphat
Jethro
Linus
Moses
Phineas
Rufus
Samson

Donkey
Baalam

Duck
Jemimah

Fish
Ishmael
Jonah

Eve

Think of it—Adam had all the creative license in the world (literally) to name his new helpmate, and he chose Eve "because she would become the mother of all the living" (Genesis 3:20). The first-ever female name in all time, space, and history has proved to be suitably timeless in its vast appeal. Smart, streamlined, genteel, and elegant, Eve's strength (like one-syllable sisters Claire, Hope, Grace, and Rose) lies in her simplicity. From the Hebrew *Havva* ("life, life-giving"), Eve is also notorious for persuading her husband to eat the fruit from the Tree of the Knowledge of Good and Evil, precipitating the fall of humankind (Genesis 2:17). The First Couple's tragic lack of judgment hasn't hurt Adam's popularity as a name; Why should it stand in the way of your bestowing this classy designation on your baby girl? FYI: The derivative Eva is showing signs of becoming the next Anna. Eve can't be far behind.

Faith

And Other Virtue Names

One-syllable names have much to recommend themselves in their sleek, straightforward approach without a lot of fuss and frills. And virtue names, now experiencing a heady revival, are even better because they suggest wonderful things about their bearers (and their parents!). Faith, once considered a bit Puritanical (after all, they were the ones who first used it), is now in the haut couture level of fashionable names. Sophisticated and polished, Faith is also warm and friendly, resonant of its obvious meaning, "belief in God." This name honors your own deeply held convictions, as does the rising star Grace.

Slightly less lofty than its avowed sister Faith, Grace is selected more and more often for its simple beauty and charm, purity and prettiness, not to mention as a reflection of gratitude to God for his abundant gifts, including sweet baby girls! Gracie adds another syllable, and ups the cute factor as well. (Warning: Grace is hot, and there is no telling when or if such a name will overheat.)

Classic Hope is catching up with Grace in some spheres, although it likely won't reach those stellar heights of popularity. By blessing your baby with this elegant, understated name, you are in essence wishing her the strength and optimism to persevere whatever may come and to base her life on the one true source of hope.

Other Virtuous Contenders

- Charity
- Chastity
- Joy
- Justice
- Mercy

- Prudence
- Purity
- Truth
- Verity

Hannah

Just a short decade ago, Hannah seemed unthinkable in its radically Jewish image and soft, plain sound. Today Hannah is completely out of control, speeding recklessly from obscurity to the dizzying vistas of the number-two spot on the charts. The most famous Hannah (Hebrew, meaning "gracious," and "she who is blessed by God") was a remarkable woman who endured years of infertility. When God answered her fervent prayers with a son, Samuel, Hannah made good on her promise and gave her much-wanted child back to God for a lifetime of service to him (1 Samuel 1–2). This gentle classic is delicate, old-fashioned, and homespun. But—and this is a biggie—Hannah is far, far too popular to choose at this point. Unless you have a deeply personal, compelling reason (see "Why We Named Our Daughter Hannah"), or if you truly don't have a problem with your daughter having the same name as her three best friends, don't go down that overcrowded path.

Why We Named Our Daughter Hannah

We are committed Christians and always knew we wanted to have a biblical name for our daughter. Proverbs 22:1 says, "A good name is more desirable than great riches." Believing that a name is a precious gift that should be prayerfully and carefully chosen, we picked the name Hannah for our daughter. Since we struggled with infertility for many years, I (Denise) especially related to Hannah's story in the Old Testament. She, too, longed for a child and poured out her heart to the Lord. He heard her cries, answering her heart's desire for a baby. God answered our prayers by blessing us with a wonderful daughter. As a testimony to him, we gave her the name Hannah. It has given us many opportunities to share God's grace and goodness with others. It is no coincidence that Hannah's name, literally translated, means "grace."

—John and Denise VandenAkker

Jemimah

If only pancakes were banned in North America, this adorable name would stand half a chance. Rosenkratz and Satran are with me on this one: "Jemimah is a name we would love to liberate," they confess in *The Last Word on First Names*. This soft Hebrew name boasts a radically different image in England, where the upper crustiest of earls and counts confer it on their silver-spooned babies. Sadly, like other Brit hits—Harriet, Beatrice, and Eugenia to name a few—Jemimah seems quite implausible in the New World. Hopefully, some intrepid baby-namers out there will refuse to be victimized by imitation maple syrup and use this appealing, gentle name for their daughter. If you are such a valiant spirit, take heart from Jemimah's positive biblical mention as the firstborn daughter of Job's second family: "Nowhere in all the land were there found women as beautiful as Job's daughters, and their father granted them an inheritance along with their brothers" (Job 42:15).

Jerusha

Little is known about Jerusha, a queen of Judah mentioned briefly in 2 Kings 15:33. But because she was both the wife of a godly king (Uzziah), and more tellingly, the mother of one (Jotham), we can quite safely speculate that Jerusha was also a woman who worshiped the one true God. Meaning "inheritance," this soft and lovely Hebrew name is a decidedly fascinating, offbeat choice. One of Billy Graham's daughters, Gigi Tchividjian, gave this rare treasure to her youngest child.

Joely

Joely, made up by Connie Stevens and Eddie Fisher for their baby (actress Joely Fisher) to honor fellow actor Joel Grey, is a feminized version of Joel. They were both ahead of and behind the times in their choice: In Victorian days, girls were routinely given such formal designations as Jamesina and Phillipa; before that Charlotte and Edwina had their day in the Edwardian sun. In the nineties, Sydney has been in high demand by parents searching for a gender-neutral name. Joely is all tomboyish charm, bubbling over with high-energy, fun, and a little offbeat kick. Sharing the same tonal ring as Kailey, Bailey, and others, Joely ("Jehovah is God") is a terrific way to honor a beloved family member named Joel or to recall to mind the great minor prophet who preached a message of repentance and forgiveness to Judah in his rousing book.

Jordan

Climbing steadily up the charts, Jordan has already overheated in some pockets of the country. But if you have investigated your own sphere and found it curiously lacking, by all means nab Jordan while the gettin's good! More linen than lace, this stylish alias would suit a soccer forward as well as it would a tea-party-loving girly-girl. If people accuse you of using a trendy name, remind them that Jordan has roots as archaic as its namesake river, the most prominent in the Bible. Bordering the exotic, lovely nation of Jordan on one side and Israel on the other, the seventy-mile-long river is where a number of pivotal biblical events took place, including the Israelites renewal of their covenant with God before entering the Promised Land, and Jesus' baptism. If you feel you must, Jordie and Jori could serve as shortie options, or to add flounce, Jordana is a pretty, less-used version.

Jubilee

Jubilee is not a person, a place, or even a virtue; it's an idea—God's wondrously liberating idea set forth in the book of Leviticus. The Year of Jubilee was to be celebrated every fifty years. It included forgiving all debts, freeing all slaves, and returning to its original owners all land that had been sold. Imagine the joy of a slave set free or that of a poverty-stricken person given interest-free assistance and work. That hope-filled elation is what the name Jubilee evokes, a sense of making a fresh start and having mistakes met with merciful kindness instead of harsh judgment. Though you won't find it in many baby-name books, Jubilee is nonetheless catching on as a girl's name. Parents of faith are attracted to such an abundance of gladness and grace.

Julia

The feminine version of Julius, Julia has a history dating back to Caesar's reign. Timeless, gorgeous, and as polished as a sterling silver tea set, Julia is a bona fide classic. Certainly this Latin-rooted moniker isn't underused: It's holding steady in the low thirties with girlfriends Rebecca and Anna. But because of its illustrious history as a name belonging to many saints and martyrs, not to mention one of Paul's myriad of friends and supporters (Romans 16:15), it still sounds distinctive. Supermodel Vendela named her baby girl Julia because she wanted her to have a more accessible name than her own. And of course, mega movie star Julia Roberts continues to give this name a high profile.

Keturah / Keliah

If you want your child to be the only one in her class—possibly her hometown—with a rare biblical name, look no farther than this duo of scarce gems. As Abraham's third wife (after Sarah and Hagar), Keturah proved to be exceedingly fertile, bearing the patriarch six sons (Genesis 25:1-2). This unusual alias may also appeal to parents drawn to *ah* names such as Hannah, Leah, and Sarah. Still in the realm of blissful obscurity is Keliah (Keh-LEE-yah), spelled Kelaiah in some translations. The biblical bearer of this name was a descendant of a priest, a Levite man in the time of Ezra (Ezra 10:23). Keliah has lots going for it—charm, prettiness, three syllables, and an upbeat meaning, "victory." This Hebrew name will work for those of you who enjoy concocting new baby names in your spare time. Keliah sounds like a hybrid invention of pleasing vowels and friendly sound combinations, but it is anchored in a strong biblical antecedent.

Ten Bible Gender Benders

Feminizations of Masculine Names

- Abra* (Abraham)
- Davida (David)
- Eliya* (Elijah)
- Gabrielle (Gabriel)
- Isaaca (Ee-SAH-kah; Isaac)
- Joely* (Joel)
- Jonatha (Jonathan)
- Phillipa (Philip)
- Simone, Simona (Simon)
- Yona (Jonah)

*Profiles found elsewhere in *"A" Is for Adam*

Leah

Sophisticated without being snobbish, sweet without becoming sugary, Leah is one of those rare names that convey both fortitude and flair. Leah calls to mind a woman who, though not overly concerned with her appearance, still exudes a clean and classic look. In the love triangle of Jacob, Leah, and her sister Rachel, Leah was definitely the odd one out. Placed in the unenviable position of trying to wrench her husband's attention away from the nubile Rachel, Leah tried to gain Jacob's love by giving him sons. Though this tactic didn't work, Leah was still blessed with seven children. A splendid selection for parents who want a unique—though not oddly so—identity for their baby girl.

Lily

Just as the rainbow is a symbol of the God who keeps his promises, so the lily is a lovely reminder that the Creator does not ignore those who depend on him. Many songs, poems, and sermons have been devoted to the message of the lily, which Jesus used so effectively in his teaching about worry. "And why do you worry about clothes? See how the lilies of the field grow. They do not labor or spin. Yet I tell you that not even Solomon in all his splendor was dressed like one of these" (Matthew 6:28-29). By giving your child this delicate flower name, you will have many opportunities to explain that her name is an emblem of God's provision and care. Overflowing with rich meaning, Lily is also infused with a singular beauty and grace. Currently hovering in that golden sphere between faddish and bizarre, Lily is going places fast. Young actor Chris O'Donnell's firstborn is Lily Anne.

Lydia

Unless you are a huge Marx Brothers fan and therefore encumbered with the image of Lydia the Tattooed Lady, this gentle, old-fashioned name is a winner on several levels. It evokes the images of a wellborn young lady wearing an empire waist gown (thank you, Jane Austen), a polished woman of the arts (it means "cultured one"), and the gracious member of the early church who opened her home to Timothy, Paul, and Silas on their missionary journey. The Lydia mentioned in Acts 16:11-15 was a wealthy businesswoman who sold purple cloth, a valuable and expensive commodity. She was Paul's first convert in Macedonia, and the members of her family followed her and were baptized. This Greek name is being picked up by an increasing number of parents who are attracted to the classic stature and biblical backbone of say, Abigail and Hannah, yet want something out of the ordinary event.

Why We Named Our Daughter Lydia

Both of us wanted a name that was not overly popular. Not only is Lydia an uncommon name, but we were impressed by the virtuous seller of purple in the book of Acts. This woman was hard working and industrious and apparently had the gift of hospitality. At the age of six, our sweet Lydia has not had much of an opportunity to host guests of her own, but her hard-working servant nature already is apparent in service to her family. Shortly after her mother arrived home with our fourth child, Lydia, feeling that her mother had been on her feet for too long, offered to do the dishes and laundry. She proceeded to do all of the dishes by hand and wash two loads of laundry. She is certainly following in the steps of her biblical namesake. It has been our prayer that we would pick for each of our children a name that has been written in the Lamb's Book of Life.

—*Timothy and Deborah Daniels*

Magdalene

Magdalene originated as a derivative of a place name, Magdala, a town on the shore of Galilee. Mary Magdalene was a devout disciple of Christ who served him with a thankful, childlike faith. After Jesus drove seven demons from her (Luke 8:2), this grateful woman responded by following her healer everywhere, even to the cross, where she and John were among the only believers with the courage to stay with him. Three days later on her way to anoint Jesus' body, Mary Magdalene was the first to see the risen Savior (John 20:14). Her story of redemption and wholehearted service is enough to recommend the stately Magdalene, but beyond that the name holds great possibility. The French version is the ultrahot Madeline, and the shortened form Maggie is one of the cutest, most likable nicknames around. Call her Maggie until she's collecting social security if you wish, but gift your daughter with this unusual, elegant, and spiritually meaningful, formal name.

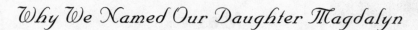

Why We Named Our Daughter Magdalyn

As we contemplated names, we were really searching for something uncommon yet easy to pronounce. We liked the name Margaret, especially since that was my grandmother's name, and we were also drawn to the newer-sounding Madeline. The nickname Maggie was more pleasing to us than Maddie, and since our firstborn, Gabriel, had a Bible name, we wanted to have our second child follow suit. Our daughter is truly growing into her name. She is our strong, yet soft little Magdalyn.

—*Steve and Amy Quakkelaar*

Mary

Mary is the biggest blockbuster girl's name of all time. Even in New Testament days, there were four Marys mentioned in Scripture, including Mary, the mother of Jesus. Among early Christians there were oodles of girls bearing this Greek version of the Hebrew Miriam, but for several hundred years the name was thought to be too holy to be worn by a mere mortal. Around the twelfth century, Christians started designating it once again for their daughters, and Mary reigned supreme as the number one girls' name for centuries. Finally in the late 1940s, Linda booted Mary from her entrenched spot at the top. Yet even today, she hangs on in the top fifty. The reason for Mary's peerless popularity is that parents through the ages have wanted to honor the Nazarene teenager who bore the Son of God. Despite her tender age (likely around thirteen), Mary possessed a bedrock faith that enabled her to give a swift and uncompromising reply to the angel Gabriel's shocking announcement of her pregnancy. " 'I am the Lord's servant,' Mary answered. 'May it be to me as you have said' " (Luke 1:38).

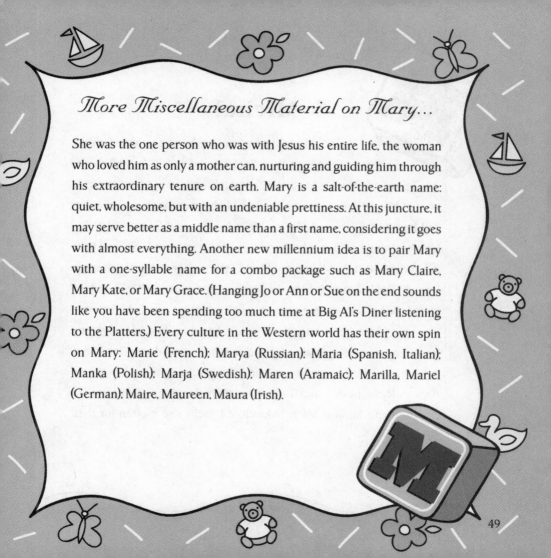

More Miscellaneous Material on Mary...

She was the one person who was with Jesus his entire life, the woman who loved him as only a mother can, nurturing and guiding him through his extraordinary tenure on earth. Mary is a salt-of-the-earth name: quiet, wholesome, but with an undeniable prettiness. At this juncture, it may serve better as a middle name than a first name, considering it goes with almost everything. Another new millennium idea is to pair Mary with a one-syllable name for a combo package such as Mary Claire, Mary Kate, or Mary Grace. (Hanging Jo or Ann or Sue on the end sounds like you have been spending too much time at Big Al's Diner listening to the Platters.) Every culture in the Western world has their own spin on Mary: Marie (French); Marya (Russian); Maria (Spanish, Italian); Manka (Polish); Marja (Swedish); Maren (Aramaic); Marilla, Mariel (German); Maire, Maureen, Maura (Irish).

Michal

Princess Michal had it rough. She was in love with the very man her father, King Saul, wanted to kill. And when she was given to David as his first wife (a cunning move on Saul's part; he wanted his girl to ensnare the enemy), Michal was torn between father and husband. She saved David's life at least once (1 Samuel 19:11), but later her adoration of her husband turned to contempt (2 Samuel 6:20-22). A dramatic tale, Michal and David's story resonates with romance, bravery, and heartbreak. Since her male counterpart, Michael, has dominated the boys' charts for more than half a century, it's Michal's turn to grace girls' birth certificates in the new millennium. Michal is vigorous, feisty, and surprisingly alluring and feminine considering its all-boy reputation. Today's parents are increasingly turning to such boy wonders as Ryan, Kevyn, and Tanner for their daughters. Why not the beautiful and biblical Michal? Modern Israelis use it often for their baby girls.

Miriam / Marah

Children will be well acquainted with the story of Miriam, who watched over her baby brother Moses as he floated along the river Nile in a basket. The quick-thinking girl grew up into a leader and prophetess. As a songwriter and musician, she led the Israelite women in dancing as she sang her lyrics of worship (Exodus 15:20-21) From the Hebrew ("bitter," "mistress of the sea," "desired and longed for"), Miriam is a refined and lovely name, distinctively biblical yet very accessible for today. Short forms include the Star-Trekish Miri and the homespun Mimi. Marah is a place name, sort of. After crossing the Red Sea, Moses led the people of Israel to the Wilderness of Shur. When their first base camp failed to yield anything but foul water, the grumbling Israelites renamed the place Marah, meaning "bitter" (Exodus 15:23). Certainly the name is much sweeter than its meaning. Sharing an exotic mystique with the hot, hip Maya, Marah is also the name of an African river.

The Perfect Baby-Name Finder
Magazine-Type Quiz

Here's how this works: You and your spouse have a few names on the short list, each vying for the grand prize of being given to your precious, kicking, unborn child. There is no clear winner yet, although on any given day one or both of you think you have made your final decision. Of course the process of designating a social identification tag to a human being for about eighty years of use is no small matter. Certainly there will be bickering: Never in the history of mankind have there been two people who have both loved a baby name with equal passion. But there will also be plenty of laughs. (I chortled uncontrollably when the family name "Bilk" was brought up for discussion.) So it has come down to this, the merit system, where points are awarded or subtracted depending on the answer to the question. When one name emerges with the most points, Eureka! You've hit the jackpot.

1. Pick a name off your list and give it 20 points if you love it beyond all reason, logic, and persuasion.

2. Add 10 points if:

   a. You have a dear family member with the same name (5 if it's just a great-aunt you never met).
   b. The name expresses one or both of your ethnic backgrounds.
   c. The name has a great biblical role model or spiritual lesson.
   d. It shows up in at least one favorite book or song.
   e. It has a beautiful, profound, or personal meaning (for example, not Hulda, which means "to dig").

3. Subtract 10 points if it:

   a. Is among the top fifteen baby names. (Warning: flammable baby names!)
   b. Is a totally newfangled, nouveau name. (Hello, Kailey.)
   c. Is a nickname name. (Instead of Maggie, use Magdalene and call her Maggie. She will thank you someday.)
   d. Clashes with your last name (although that can be debated!).
   e. Sounds like something that washed up on Sunset Beach. (Beware supersudsy soap names like Jagger, Bliss, and Thorne!)

4. Add 'em up.

Naomi

Mellifluous, tender, and happily underused, Naomi is a name full of bonuses. Not only is it quite rare—even in Jewish cultures—Naomi brings with it the added benefit of a wonderful biblical role model. After she became a widow, Naomi headed back to Israel, alone and destitute save the presence of Orpah and Ruth, foreign girls from despised Moab. Naomi was a woman with abundant kindness and a huge heart. Even though she needed them keenly, she advised her daughters-in-law to return to Moab, for their futures looked brighter there than in Israel. How many mothers-in-law would inspire weeping at the prospect of leaving them forever? Naomi did (Ruth 1:9-10). No surprise that she passed on her faith to Ruth, who embraced it whole-heartedly. Though Naomi is a Hebrew name ("pleasant, delightful," "my sweetness"), it has a definite global-village ring to it. (Prime example: British supermodel Naomi Campbell, who is of African descent.)

Noa

That boys' names are now wide open for selection as girls' names is well documented in these pages and other sources. Just glance at any pre-school roster and you could very well find a female Cameron or Dylan. TV mastermind David E. Kelley has recently named two female characters Glenn and Jeremy. With that in mind, here's another gender-neutral alias to consider: Noa. This Hebrew name isn't simply the feminization of Noah. In Numbers 26:33, Noah is listed as the daughter of Zelophehad. (Remember him? Hmm. Me neither.) And while the spelling *Noah* shows up in many translations, the alternate *Noa* has been used for girls since before the Iron Age. At any rate, baby-name experts are starting to warm up to Noa. "Looks—and sounds—very today," praises Joal Ryan. Noa was the name of Itzhak Rabin's grand-daughter who spoke so movingly about her slain grandfather at the funeral of Israel's former prime minister.

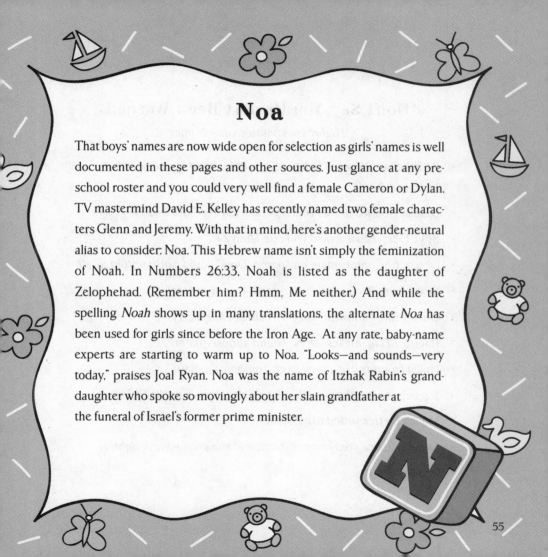

Don't Say You Haven't Been Warned

Highly Unadvisable Girls' Names

- Bathsheba *(awkward when the whole bathing story comes up in Sunday school)*
- Basmat *(sounds like a French person saying "bath mat")*
- Bitya *("Hey Bitya, who'd you bite lately?")*
- Dorcas *(the unfortunate nickname "Dork" could cause untold grief)*
- Efrat *(the suffix "rat" is a bit too redolent of rodent)*
- Gomer *(the gumpiest name this side of Mayberry)*
- Haggar *("Hag" makes "Dork" sound almost quaint)*
- Hulda *(sounds like a very large Teutonic woman)*
- Jezebel *(you might as well call your daughter "Cruella DeVille")*
- Milcah *(better suited to a bovine)*
- Ophrah *(there's only one of those, and she's not your daughter)*
- Uzza *(uh, no)*

Phoebe

This shimmering name ("bright, radiant") is at once as ancient as the early church and strikingly modern. Phoebe was an important member of the Corinthian church, a wealthy woman who supported Paul's ministry. Some scholars believe she may possibly be the author of the book of Hebrews. The apostle Paul glowingly commended her to the Roman church, saying, "She has been a great help to many people, including me" (Romans 16:2). Many great writers, from the Bard to J. D. Salinger, have bestowed this luminous name on key characters. Nature lovers will know that Phoebe is the name of a lovely bird that got its name by singing "fee-bee" at regular intervals. Caveat: Fellow Gen Xers may think you actually got the idea from the sweet, ditzy character Phoebe on the sitcom *Friends*. Oh, well. The show can't be in reruns forever, can it?

Priscilla

The Pilgrims really dug this name (one even sailed on the *Mayflower*), and indeed Priscilla has a rather formal, colonial ambience (it actually means "of ancient lineage"). In *The Baby Name Survey Book* by Bruce Lansky and Barry Sinrod, one hundred thousand people were polled for their gut responses to various names. Here's how this Latin name fared: "Most people picture Priscilla as a prude who is pretty, feminine, uptight, but not above flirting." Hmm. Priscilla should be freed from her starchy corsets and coquettish ways. Think of it as a quaint, refined kind of name with deep roots in American history, and perhaps you will warm up to its delicacy and classic stature. The biblical Priscilla was also a gem: She and her husband, Aquila, early Christians in Corinth, were a great help to the apostle Paul (Acts 18:2). Certainly this would be a far more original choice than Marissa or Vanessa. Cilla is the charming shortie.

Rachel

It's safe to say the patriarch Jacob was madly in love with Rachel, his intended bride. A steep dowry of seven years' labor would have sent most suitors running for the hills, but not this smitten lad: "So Jacob served seven years to get Rachel, but they seemed like only a few days to him because of his love for her" (Genesis 29:20). Rachel was beautiful, and she was the wife he adored despite her many years of infertility. (In the end, she bore Jacob two sons, Joseph and Benjamin.) Rachel is also one of the most widely used Bible names for girls, currently anchored at number fifteen on the charts. As lovely as its biblical bearer, Rachel appeals to parents from all ethnic backgrounds. Though this gentle Hebrew designation ("little lamb") has definitely reached the saturation point, I can't dismiss it—it's just too strong, attractive, classic, and intelligent. If originality is not your aim, go for it.

Golden Oldies:
Charts from the Days of Your Great-Grandma, Your Grandma, Your Mom, and You

1900	1925	1945	1970
1. Mary	1. Mary	1. Mary	1. Jennifer
2. Helen	2. Dorothy	2. Linda	2. Lisa
3. Anna	3. Betty	3. Barbara	3. Kimberly
4. Margaret	4. Margaret	4. Patricia	4. Michelle
5. Ruth	5. Helen	5. Carol	5. Angela
6. Elizabeth	6. Ruth	6. Maria	6. Maria
7. Marie	7. Doris	7. Sandra	7. Amy
8. Florence	8. Virginia	8. Nancy	8. Melissa
9. Bertha	9. Elizabeth	9. Sharon	9. Mary
10. Gladys	10. Evelyn/ Mildred	10. Susan	10. Tracy

Raomi

Here is a sparkling idea for those parents who are willing to scale mountain peaks and dredge the deepest rivers for something so singular, so inventive, only their peerless progeny could pull it off: Raomi. This Aramaic name (spelled *Reumah* in many translations) has a nice global-village backbeat, a United Colors of Benetton quality that immediately evokes images of a savvy woman decked out in khaki who has just returned from Nepal, Java, or some similarly exotic destination. Raomi would definitely look terrific on a passport if you are planning a family career in cross-cultural missions or diplomacy. Having said that, you must know that neither the biblical reference nor the meaning hold much in the way of spiritual nurturing: Raomi was Abraham's sister-in-law, sort of, who bore his bro Nahor four sons (Genesis 22:24), and her name means "antelope." Ray or Rao are sporty shorties.

Rebekah

Rebekah, like her future daughter-in-law Rachel, was also noted for her great beauty, and she and the patriarch Isaac were a love match (Genesis 24). Rebekah is one of the most obviously biblical names, especially with its proper Old Testament spelling as opposed to the Anglicized Rebecca. The latter spelling is a perennial bestseller, so to speak, as it has endured since the seventeenth century as a favorite girl's name. The biblical spelling, though, for our purposes, is much more distinctive and creative. The Hebrew form is the alluring Rivkah, and the most modern nickname is Becca or Bekah (Becky graduated in the class of '87). When a name suits a basketball star (Rebecca Lobo) as well as several heroines in classic literature (see *Ivanhoe, Rebecca,* etc.), you know it's trend resistant.

Why We Named Our Daughter Rebekah

We chose the name Rebekah for its meaning ("to be bound to God"), for its spelling and Hebrew origin, and to honor the biblical Rebekah's display of courage, character, and independence. As Rebekah was chosen by God to be Isaac's wife, so we feel God has chosen our Rebekah for something special. We want our little girl to grow into a strong and confident woman, and her namesake truly demonstrated those qualities and more. She was a woman who had the courage to take risks by leaving her home and marrying a stranger from an unknown land! Most important, it's our desire for her to become bound to God as she witnesses his boundless love, grace, and mercy. On a lighter note, we simply love the name. We wanted to keep the Hebrew spelling to indicate its national and ethnic origin and to allow it to help point our Rebekah to the Scriptures.

—*Mike and Connie Guy*

Ruth

Emerging as number seven on the American top ten in 1872, and having a successful run for over fifty years, Ruth is starting to sound new again in the wake of the one-syllable revival (Rose, Jane, Grace). As a social identification, Ruth ("friendship") evokes a cool-headed woman who is nurturing and kind to a fault, and in terms of being a role model, the biblical Ruth is among the best. She embraced faith in Israel's God and displayed tenacious loyalty to her mother-in-law, Naomi, uttering these lovely words: "Where you go I will go, and where you stay I will stay. Your people will be my people and your God my God" (Ruth 1:16). Ruth refused to be parted from Naomi and was committed to her welfare even after remarrying the wealthy Boaz. God blessed her for her faithfulness: Ruth became the great-grandmother of David and an ancestor of Jesus. Ruthie is just as cute as Gracie and is the name of the winsome little girl on TV's *7th Heaven*.

Sarah

Sarah means "princess," but it really doesn't have that kind of negative, pampered image. Next to Hannah, Sarah is the most popular Bible name for girls: It seems to have signed a long-term lease on the top five. In Genesis 21:1-7, Sarah conceived and gave birth to Abraham's son Isaac when she was at least ninety years old, making her the mother of the Jewish race. Choosing Sarah would be less than a trailblazing move at this point. But if you've wanted to name a baby girl Sarah since grade school, there are a few things you can do to freshen it up: Attach it to a hip one-syllable name, like Harry Connick Jr. did with his daughter, Sara Kate. Sarah Rose is as pretty as a picture, and Sarah Jane is sweet and quaint. Or put Sarah on the birth certificate, but call her something more interesting, like the cute, farm-girlish Sadie, an actual antique nickname of Sarah's, or the world-beat sounding Sari.

Selah

Hip-hop singer Lauryn Hill is not only a musical trailblazer, she also pioneered a couple of all-new baby names, including her choice of Selah for her daughter (see also Zion). The music connection is abundantly clear for Hill and other musical types who want a melodious, rare name for their daughter. According to the *Life Application Bible* (NIV), the word *Selah* occurs seventy-one times in the Psalms and three times in Habakkuk. "Though its precise meaning is unknown, it was most likely a musical sign. Three suggestions are: (1) it was a musical direction to singers and orchestra to play forte or crescendo; (2) it was a signal to lift up hands or voice in worship; and (3) it was a word like *amen* meaning 'so be it,' or *hallelujah* meaning 'praise the Lord.'" All of these possibilities are positive, and so is the fact that you would be getting in on the ground floor with a very appealing, vivid name.

Lorilee's Top Ten Girls' Names

These are my picks for the names that will hold the most appeal for today's parents. My criteria is based on great spiritual application, class, creativity, and a fresh and interesting sound. You won't find any of these names on the top one hundred (yeah!), which makes them all the more appealing. If you want a name in that wonderful, blissful realm between overused and odd-ball, consult the following:

- Acacia
- Clementine
- Dinah
- Eve
- Faith

- Lily
- Magdalene
- Phoebe
- Shiloh
- Tabitha

Shiloh

This vigorous Hebrew name has that windblown "earth and sky" thing going for it, but it is definitely fresher than Dakota, Sierra, or Savannah. Shiloh was the focal point of Israel's worship, the religious center of the nation where the tabernacle and the ark of the covenant were kept (Joshua 18:1). This holy place was centrally located in the Promised Land to make it convenient for people to attend special worship services and feasts. Hannah prayed for a baby there, and God called her son, Samuel, at Shiloh as well. The meaning of the name varies: Some sources cite it to be "tranquility" while others say "the gift is God's" or "God's gift." Any name ending in the *oh* sound is vivid, fun, and wonderfully distinctive. Perhaps with the rise of Milo as a trendy boys' name, this vowel sound is making inroads. It's up to the adventurous among you to break new ground with this cheerful place name.

Why We Named Our Daughter Shiloh

My husband and I were having a difficult time agreeing on a name for our baby. Our boy's name was set in stone, but we could not think of a girl's name we both liked. Taylor, Shayne, Lydia . . . they were all suggested, but nothing that we *both* wanted. Then one day in casual conversation the name Shiloh came up. We both loved it right away and decided that it was the name we wanted for our daughter. Fortunately after all that, we *did* have a girl and were able to use the name! We later found out that Shiloh is a Hebrew word meaning "tranquility." How often we have prayed that Shiloh could be more like the meaning of her name, but then again, that's a pretty huge request for a two-year-old!

—*Jeff and Lori Edwardh*

Shoshanah/Susanna

Here are a couple of "now" variations on the Susan theme: Susanna is noted in Luke 8:3 as being a woman who traveled with Jesus and his disciples, supporting his ministry. The text also says she had been "cured of evil spirits and diseases" and was "the manager of Herod's household." An obscure reference, perhaps, but it's there! Susanna is a sterling-silver classic name, one that is surprisingly underused. It has a definite Pilgrim patina, a colonial charm as enduring as fellow *Mayflower* voyagers Priscilla, Sarah, and Katherine. Shoshanah, the Hebrew version, boasts a whopping three *H*'s and injects verve into Susannah's rather reserved veneer. Both names mean "lily," and either one is completely yours for the taking as a rare and valuable find.

Tabitha

Despite the fact that this rather obscure treasure means "gazelle," Tabitha seems forever aligned with the feline, perhaps because of the nickname Tabby. It also seems to carry an aura of mystery, no doubt due to the name's affiliation with the little girl from the classic sitcom *Bewitched,* which today's baby-namers probably watched with after-school snacks. Parents who bypass Tabitha for this reason are missing the fact that it has a much more illustrious history than TV reruns. In Acts 9:36, Tabitha was the extremely well regarded disciple who "was always doing good and helping the poor." When she died, those whose lives she had touched with her kindness mourned her, and they later rejoiced when Peter raised her from the dead. This charming, under-used name deserves a life beyond *Nick at Nite.*

Sister Acts

Baby name experts agree that "matching" the names of all of your children is a good idea. There is something disconcerting about a sibling group whose names veer wildly from one another. For instance, consider a girl named Emma—a nice classic, tasteful, literary name. If you named her baby sister Brandy (just to choose the silliest name I can think of), it would clash—badly. Throw in a gender-neutral name like Dylan for sister number three, and worlds are colliding. Besides, you have your own personal baby-naming likes and dislikes, proclivities and predispositions. Every name has a few others in the same family. (If you do happen to adore Brandy and are now upset with me, your next choices should be made in the frothy princess pool where Brittney and Krystal are splashing around.) The majority of people choose from the same pond of five hundred names. It's a fact. Here are a few similar puddles from which to choose a coordinating sister name for your next baby. (If you are naming your pet ducks, turn to page 28.)

- *Classic Biblical Babes:* Abigail, Anna, Elizabeth, Esther, Leah, Lydia, Mary, Rachel, Rebekah, Sarah

- *We-Are-Marching-to-Zion Band:* Hadassah, Jerusha, Noa, Raomi, Shiloh, Shoshanna, Zion, Zorah
- *Only-One-of-a-Kind-Will-Do Progeny:* Drusilla, Eliya, Keturah, Raomi, Seraiah
- *Tomboyish Charm Chicks:* Michal, Noa, Seth, Shiloh, Joely, Jordan
- *Mayflower Misses:* Lydia, Priscilla, Susannah
- *Quirky, Arty, Cutie-Patootie Pack:* Abra, Ariel, Chloe, Dinah, Eden, Phoebe, Tabitha
- *We-Set-the-Trends-Trailblazers:* Clementine, Keliah, Lily, Magdalene, Phoebe, Tabitha
- *Soft and Sweet Sisters:* Damaris, Deborah, Hannah, Miriam, Ruth
- *Elegant and Stylish Sibs:* Eve, Faith, Hope (though not as Faith's sister. Virtue overkill!), Julia
- *Simple Prairie Charm Children:* Abigail, Anna, Grace, Sarah
- Earth and Sky Sisters: Acacia, Ariel, Eden, Moriah, Shiloh
- *Global-Village Tribe:* Naomi, Noa, Raomi (although not as Naomi's sister), Tamar, Zorah

Tamar

Tamar is strong, rich, and powerful, suggesting a woman who is destined to be a great leader. Three biblical women bore this name: the wife of Er, son of Judah (Genesis 38:6) and an ancestor of Jesus; a "beautiful" daughter of David with a tragic story (2 Samuel 13:1; 1 Chronicles 3:9); and a daughter of Absalom (2 Samuel 14:27). This creative, rather exotic name is commonly used in Israel and is gaining ground among American Jews wanting to get in touch with their Hebrew roots. Meaning "graceful Palm tree," Tamar is by no means limited to people of Jewish descent. African-American actor Meshach Taylor used it for his daughter, and I predict others of all ethnic backgrounds will soon wake up to Tamar's charisma and energy. Add an *A* and you get the more commonly heard Tamara. Note: If you are going to give your daughter a name with such fortitude, don't dilute it by calling her Tammy. Taye sounds more appropriate for today's girls.

Five Tips for Better Baby Naming

1. Honor someone you love if at all possible. Can you imagine telling your son stories of fishing with your grandpa? Even better, make your child a namesake of your beloved relative or friend.

2. Always use a formal first name instead of a nickname. If you love and adore the name Maddy, give your daughter a longer, more formal name like Madeline on her birth certificate. You are not, I repeat not, being original by shortening a well-established name!

3. Don't touch alternate spellings with a ten-foot pole. People think it's cute—not too mention creative—when they call their daughter Britnee or Shelagh or Krisstall. It won't be too cute when she respells her name seven thousand times a year.

4. Mix syllables for a nice rhythm. Usually names sound best when all three slots have a different syllable mix. For instance, Tyler Jeremiah Smith sounds more rhythmic than Ty John Smith.

5. Don't let Mom choose the girl's name and Dad the boy's. It's a give-and-take process, and since a child is part of both parents, his name should ideally reflect both.

Zion

And pushing the envelope even further is Zion. Choosing this Hebrew name meaning "protected place" would be a bold move—not for the faint of heart among you. Zion—dwelling place of the Lord (Joel 3:21)—is another name for Jerusalem, the capital city of God's chosen people and the ancestral home of David, Israel's greatest king. It was intended to be a center of worship and a symbol of justice to all people. Because of its association with Zionists, who fought to create their own homeland in Palestine in the 1940s, Zion sounds radical, warrior-like, and not altogether feminine in the traditional sense. But this name can also represent a bold and uncompromising faith and a courageous hope for the future. The subject of any number of hymns and choruses, this name is perhaps best known for the rousing tune "We Are Marching to Zion." Lauryn Hill chose this for her baby son and wrote a moving song of the same name to honor him.

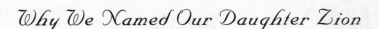

Why We Named Our Daughter Zion

My wife and I were searching for a unique biblical name that would work for a boy or a girl. A song reminded us of the word *Zion*. We began to study its biblical references. Although it was not used as a person's name in the Bible, Zion symbolizes a place of power, redemption, and grace. Zion is a promise of hope for the future. When we look at our beautiful daughter, Zion Esther, we see all of this and more.

—*Matt and Margaret Epperson*

Zorah

If you are nothing less than zealous in your quest for a unique pick, Zorah might have the "zippety doo dah" for you. *Z* names fairly bustle with enterprise and energy—next to them almost all other monikers seem sluggish. But they are usually too edgy for the masses, which means they will definitely set your child apart as being sort of out there. If it's singularity you crave, welcome to the world of *Z*'s Zorah is a place name, a village in Canaan close to the Philistine border. It was there that God called baby Samson to a life set apart for the purpose of making a difference in a worldly culture (Judges 13:5). Rooted in the Arabic and meaning "dawn," this novel name belongs to literary legend Zora Neal Hurston *(The Wedding)*. Zoe is an adorable and reasonable nickname. (By the way, if you want to pump some juice into Sarah, Zorah is a nice variation.)

Lorilee's Top Ten Boys' Names

- Abram
- Eli
- Ezra
- Isaac
- Jonah

- Levi
- Malachi
- Micah
- Reuben
- Zebedy

Aaron

A guy named Aaron will, sight unseen, strike most people favorably merely because his name elicits such a good first impression. Solid, sincere, salt-of-the-earth—that's Aaron. The biblical guy, of course, was Moses' brother, not to mention his mouthpiece. When big bro Moe shirked his speaking duties before the Lord, God suggested Aaron speak for him: "I know he can speak well....He will speak to the people for you, and it will be as if he were your mouth" (Exodus 4:14-16). Aaron thus became the first high priest in Israel. As an alias Aaron is well used (number thirty-seven), but still safely on this side of overdone. If you are drawn to the completely overheated Andrew, you would be making a more interesting, brighter choice. (Aaron, which appears to have Egyptian roots, means "enlightened, illumined.")

Abram / Abraham

This name is so cutting edge, so strong and beautiful, and full of so many profound spiritual applications that it is one of my favorites. But it does pose an immediate quandary: Which spelling do you use—Abram ("exalted father") or Abraham ("father of multitudes"), the new name God gave his man Abe after establishing a covenant with him? Well, Abram was exceedingly faithful before and after his renaming, and to the modern ear Abraham might sound too ponderous and weighty. The best benefit of this name is Abram's astonishing, bedrock trust that God would do whatever he said. Abram was already an elderly man when God promised him his descendants would be as numerous as stars. Mind-boggling, yes, but "Abram believed the LORD, and he credited it to him as righteousness" (Genesis 15:6). In this age of Jake, Mike, and Matt, Abe is a sporty, honest nickname. Bram is a more creative, earthier derivation. Avram is the beautiful Hebrew translation.

Adam

Adam is one of those golden names that age supremely well. Somehow it's all snails and puppy-dog tails on a three-year-old, yet it sounds handsome and masculine twenty, forty, and sixty years later. When a name works just as well for an aging cowboy (Adam Cartwright from *Bonanza*) as it does for a goofy, Gen X comedian (Adam Sandler), you've got flame-resistance the fire department would kill to get their hands on. Curiously, Adam's role in the fall of mankind hasn't hindered the name one bit. Perhaps people like to focus on his pre-Fall activities: caring for the Garden of Eden, naming the animals, and communing with his Creator. Key verse: "The LORD God formed man from the dust of the ground and breathed into his nostrils the breath of life" (Genesis 2:7). Note: Adam is perfect for those who don't want their boy's name shortened, no way, no how.

Amos

Amos's story reminds us that God is a God of justice who hates the oppression of the poor and expects his people to stand up for the hurting and disenfranchised. Amos, a blazing, daring, and humble fig farmer, pronounced judgment on Israel for superficial commitment and their exploitation of the poor. "But let justice roll on like a river, righteousness like a never-failing stream!" he roared in Amos 5:24. If you have a special burden for justice, this strong and vivid Hebrew name might be for you. (It actually means "burden bearer.") If the whole Amos 'n Andy thing is holding you back, get over it. That was how long ago? Like seventy years? Plus: the Famous Amos cookie thing is a sweet bonus.

Andrew

Andrew has an exceedingly macho set of possible meanings—"the virile one, manly, strong, brave"—but the name evokes a rather quiet, cerebral image. Currently number nine, Andrew has been well used among a variety of notable men, including two presidents (Johnson and Jackson) and a prince (Andrew of Great Britain). He is also the patron saint of Russia, Greece, and Scotland. Any name in the top ten should be avoided unless your love for it overpowers the fact that your son will share it with many others. Using the hip Drew for short is a differentiating idea—as is choosing one of Andrew's many foreign versions, including Andre (French), Andrei (Russian), or especially the appealing Scandinavian form, Anders. There is also a current prince with the Italian form, Andrea (ahn-DRAY-uh) of Monaco, but for obvious reasons steer clear here. In Matthew 4:18-19 the fisherman Andrew was called by Jesus as his first disciple to be a "fisher of men."

Asher

It's surprising this virile, upbeat name hasn't caught on yet, what with the popularity of surname names ending in *er* (Tyler, Hunter, Tanner, and others). Asher got his ebullient ("blessed, fortunate, happy") name through Leah, his father's wife. When she stopped having children, Leah turned to her servant Zilpah to create more children for her husband, Jacob. When Asher, Jacob's eighth son was born to Zilpah, Leah was jubilant. "How happy I am! The women will call me happy" (Genesis 30:13). Asher grew up to become one of the leaders of the twelve tribes of Israel. Ash sounds like a mannerly, manly Southern gentleman who golfs.

Benjamin

Benjamin was the youngest of Jacob's twelve sons and thus grew up to be a leader of one of the twelve tribes of Israel. When Rachel, dying in childbirth, realized he was a boy, she named him Ben-Oni, "son of my sorrows." Later the boy's doting father renamed him Benjamin, "son of my right hand" (Genesis 35:18). Many famous men have born this empathetic Hebrew alias, and some have even conferred positive qualities to the name's image: leadership from President Harrison, ingeniousness from inventor Franklin, and gentleness from Dr. Spock. Benjamin is another can't-miss moniker. At number thirty-two (with Bible pal Noah next door at number thirty-one), Ben is on the safe side of trendy, yet is still almost universally well regarded. Bonus: Benji is adorable for a tot, while the decent-sounding Ben is a great short form that will take your boy from Little League to the Ivy League and beyond.

Why We Named Our Son Benjamin

"He's such a gentle soul," I said at my son's arrival. "He's Benjamin," his daddy agreed. Granted we were a little delirious the moment we named our son, and since then we've never been able to find an etymological link between the name Benjamin and the possession of a gentle soul. Still the name has a lot going for it: an old-fashioned sturdiness we really like, plus an infinite number of potential nicknames—Ben, Benny, Ben-Jammin', and my personal favorite Where-You-Ben-All-My-Life? Best of all, there is Moses' wonderful blessing upon the tribe of Benjamin: "About Benjamin he said: 'Let the beloved of the LORD rest secure in him, for he shields him all day long, and the one the LORD loves rests between his shoulders'" (Deuteronomy 33:12).

Benjamin has grown into a boisterous toddler with a smile like sunshine and the ability to trash any living room in North America in less than sixty seconds. He seldom slows down, but at bedtime he gets sleepy enough to let us hold him close and whisper thanks and a prayer to the One who dreamed up his gentle soul—a prayer that he rest, beloved, between the shoulders of God. We call it his Ben-ediction.

—*Carolyn and Mark Arends*

Adventures in Baby Naming: Twelve Quirky, Out-There, Iconoclast Boys' Names

- Bartholomew
- Boaz*
- Cyrus*
- Ishmael
- Jotham*
- Linus

- Meshach*
- Philemon*
- Rufus*
- Theophilus
- Zebulon*
- Zion (for a boy or girl)*

*Profiles found elsewhere in "A" Is for Adam

Boaz

Parents who name their baby Boaz would be going out on a limb, but for the right family this vivid tag would be worth it. Few more worthy role models exist in Scripture. Boaz was a quiet hero, a successful businessman who put the needs of others before himself and treated family and employees alike with respect and kindness. When he became the kinsman-redeemer of his relative Ruth, he took on the responsibility of a widow and her mother-in-law. God blessed him for his integrity and goodness. Boaz's great-grandson through Ruth was none other than King David, placing this wealthy Bethlehem landowner in direct lineage to Jesus. The *Z* in Boaz infuses the name with lots of zip and personality, and the nikname Bo has a dual image: rope-swinging cowboy and friendly, outgoing athlete.

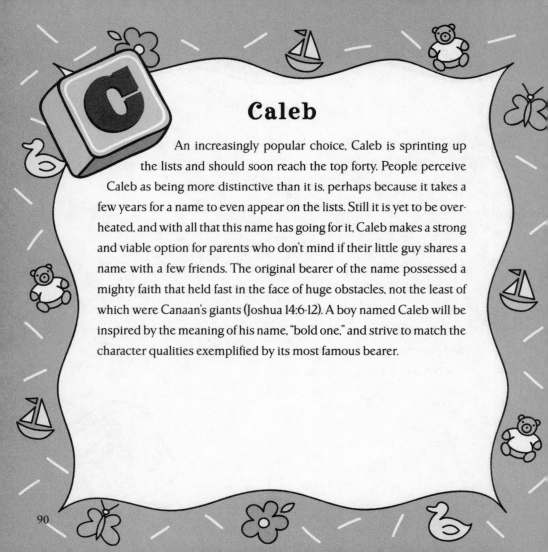

Caleb

An increasingly popular choice, Caleb is sprinting up the lists and should soon reach the top forty. People perceive Caleb as being more distinctive than it is, perhaps because it takes a few years for a name to even appear on the lists. Still it is yet to be overheated, and with all that this name has going for it, Caleb makes a strong and viable option for parents who don't mind if their little guy shares a name with a few friends. The original bearer of the name possessed a mighty faith that held fast in the face of huge obstacles, not the least of which were Canaan's giants (Joshua 14:6-12). A boy named Caleb will be inspired by the meaning of his name, "bold one," and strive to match the character qualities exemplified by its most famous bearer.

Up the Lists Faster
Than You Can Say "Jacob":
Up-and-Coming Boys' Names*

- Aaron
- Benjamin
- Caleb
- Ethan
- Gabriel

- Isaac
- Nathan
- Nathanael
- Noah
- Samuel

*All of these are profiled elsewhere in *"A" Is for Adam*

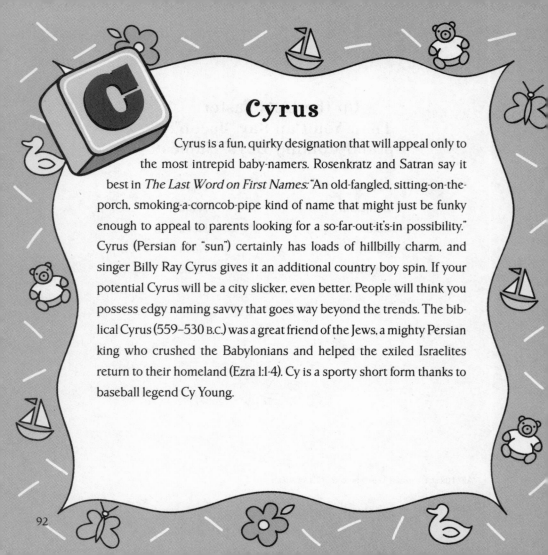

Cyrus

Cyrus is a fun, quirky designation that will appeal only to the most intrepid baby-namers. Rosenkratz and Satran say it best in *The Last Word on First Names:* "An old-fangled, sitting-on-the-porch, smoking-a-corncob-pipe kind of name that might just be funky enough to appeal to parents looking for a so-far-out-it's-in possibility." Cyrus (Persian for "sun") certainly has loads of hillbilly charm, and singer Billy Ray Cyrus gives it an additional country boy spin. If your potential Cyrus will be a city slicker, even better. People will think you possess edgy naming savvy that goes way beyond the trends. The biblical Cyrus (559–530 B.C.) was a great friend of the Jews, a mighty Persian king who crushed the Babylonians and helped the exiled Israelites return to their homeland (Ezra 1:1-4). Cy is a sporty short form thanks to baseball legend Cy Young.

Why We Named Our Son Syras

Right from the beginning, my husband loved the name Cyrus. He remembers it had something to do with Persian King Cyrus in the Bible, who was a powerful, good king, and someone who allowed the Jews to worship their God. It had connotations of strength, leadership, understanding, and tolerance. Our firstborn turned out to be a girl, so I chose the name Candace after the Egyptian queen in the Bible. Our second daughter was Odia, an abbreviation of the name in the New Testament: Euodia. Our last child was a son, so Cliff was finally able to use his chosen name for his son, Cyrus. I felt the spelling seemed so old-fashioned, so we spelled it "Syras." Syras is seventeen now and six feet tall. Sometime ago he researched the meaning of his name and discovered it to be "king." When he told me this, he stood very tall. He is our king. We adore him. I sense from him that the connotations of royalty in his name challenge him to be a better person and fill him with a sense of destiny.

—*Cliff and Willma Derksen*

Daniel

Daniel just never seems to lose its luster. The biblical guy was one of the great heroes of the faith, exemplifying an unwavering commitment to God. As a lad he was taken captive from Israel to a foreign land, where his outstanding qualities of trustworthiness and administration led him to become an advisor of kings. Daniel prayed three times a day before being thrown into the lions' den, where God protected him. He was also a major prophet who predicted the Messiah and the end times. At once as venerable as Daniel Boone's coon cap and as sophisticated as cerebral actor Daniel Day Lewis, this one is pure classic. You already know the world holds a vast surplus of Daniels—at number eleven, the name is sure to be heard frequently. But if you are looking for a safe-and-sound Bible name (with a fabulous role model to boot), Dan's your man. (Danny will work for the *Sesame Street* set.)

Darius

Hepcat Darius is surprisingly well used, belonging to a number of notables, including Darius Rucker of Hootie and the Blowfish and hockey star Darius Kasparaitus. Certainly if your son has a Persian throne in his future, this is the name for you: Three kings are mentioned in Scripture, including Darius the Mede, whose intriguing story plays out in Daniel 6. A Persian king, Darius overthrew Babylon and promoted Daniel to be his prime minister. This king had the good conscience to feel terrible when jealous staff members tricked him into throwing his favorite advisor to the lions. Darius also has a wonderful meaning: "He who upholds the good."

Also in the Key of D

- Dathan: meaning "degree or law" (Numbers 16:25)
- Debir: an Amorite king of Eglon who joined forces against Joshua (Joshua 10:3)
- Deker: one of the governors of Israel under Solomon (1 Kings 4:9)
- Demas: a fellow worker of Paul (Philemon 1:24)
- Demetrius: "is well spoken of by everyone" (3 John 12)

David

According to Tony Castle, a British baby-name writer, David was originally a Hebrew lullaby word meaning "beloved" or "darling." While that is one of sweetest bits of trivia in this book, it still doesn't inject much excitement into this perennially overused boys' name. If it's a matter of your being enthralled with the great King David, shepherd boy, slayer of giants, poet and musician extraordinaire, and a "man after God's own heart," that's one thing. He was an extraordinary, sensitive man, and his psalms reveal a deeply feeling heart. But if you just like the way it sounds, sturdy and reliable, mild and inoffensive, ask yourself this: Do I want my precious, one-of-a-kind baby boy to grow up with the same name as 25 percent of my graduating class? Today the popularity of David has calmed down to a dull roar (number sixteen). But trust me. You can do better! As a nickname, could anything be blander than Dave? Hardly.

Eli

Eli Whitney invented the cotton gin, and his first name is as clever and creative as he was. Eli ("height, ascend") is "the Max less traveled," according to Joal Ryan. Everything that made the name Max the hip, urbane choice of the last decade is also going for Eli: short, punchy, packs-an-attitude, loaded with character! If you like Ethan and Evan, consider the charming, manly, and fashionable Eli, which is much less used. In 1 Samuel 1–4, Eli's story unfolds. He judged Israel for forty years and as a high priest was kind to Hannah when she came to the temple praying in anguish for a son. Later she brought little Samuel to Eli, who turned Samuel into the finest judge in the nation's history. Eli's sons, however, were noted for their evil ways. Despite this, Eli would make a novel, vivid, and fascinating choice for your son.

Elijah

Elijah has potency, drama, courage—all the virtues that made its biblical namesake such a fearless hero of the faith. Elijah's boldness is exemplified in the spectacular story of his showdown with the Baal cultists when he gathered all the people of Israel to see for themselves what a sham Baal was. Elijah is also renowned for skipping death and traveling to heaven in a chariot of fire. This name holds enormous appeal as both a cuddly little boy's tag and a masculine, warm, and strong designation for a man. Creeping, not zooming, up the charts (a good thing), Elijah is currently hanging out at number seventy-one, an enviable position to be sure. Famous guy: actor Elijah Wood. Two-for-one bonus: Eli is the short version.

Ethan

You've got to hand it to the Puritans. They had the panache and good sense to launch such unheard-of gems as Ethan, and many wise parents have followed in their footsteps. Meaning "steadfast and firm," Ethan has a dual image—as scholarly young man on the rowing team at Yale and as a wrangler swapping stories around the campfire. Edith Wharton's troubled title character, Ethan Frome, injects some literary feel while Revolutionary War soldier Ethan Allen (of furniture fame) lends historic backbone. In 1 Kings 4:31, Ethan was named as a wise man and in 1 Chronicles 2:6 as a grandson of Judah. I predict that this handsome name—getting warmer at number thirty-six—has a future in the top ten. Bonus: Ethan is a rootsy alternative to Austin and Ryan.

Ezekiel

Only a few years ago, this wild and wooly name conjured up images of a white-bearded dude, ranting and raving in suitably oddball, prophet fashion. Now with Ezra and Elijah making their presence known, Ezekiel doesn't sound so drastic. In fact it has a great deal of mountain-man charm. (Actor Beau Bridges thought so. He bestowed this zesty name on his son a few years ago.) The biblical Ezekiel was among the young men who were taken captive from Judah to Babylon. Trained as a priest, Ezekiel was called as a prophet to the exiled believers. Among his megawatt dreams was the vision of "dry bones." Consider the NFL's Ezekiel Moore Jr. if you need another image to go on. Big plus: Zeke is only a heartbeat away from Zach, yet vastly less common.

Ezra

This up-and-coming Old Testament name brings to mind a rather grizzled mountain man, but instead of tanning a hide, he is crafting words on paper by lantern light. Ezra's association with writing is no fluke: Many noted writers have been dubbed this Hebrew name including poet Ezra Pound and children's author Ezra Jack. The biblical character was also a writer, a scribe who devoted himself to studying God's word and later teaching it to the Israelites. As a leader, he also had the moxie to join Nehemiah in starting a revival among their people. Actor Paul Reiser, who chose this offbeat name for his son, joined a growing number of baby-namers who appreciate Ezra's maverick qualities. An especially suitable pick for the baby son of a writer.

Gabriel

During your son's turbulent toddler years, you can comfort yourself with the thought that you named him after an angel. (Perhaps someday he will live up to the peace and composure that evokes!) Gabriel is poetic, handsome, accessible, masculine—no wonder it is on the rise. Though not the toughest name on the block, Gabriel is hardly wimpy either. With an athletic nickname like Gabe, your kid can confidently check fellow sporty dudes Jake and Nate into the boards at a hockey game. In the Bible, Gabriel ("God is my strength") was the archangel who appeared to Daniel, Zechariah, and most famously to Mary, when he announced that she would be the mother of the Son of God (Luke 1:26-38). Actor Gabriel Byrne and physicist Gabriel Fahrenheit are other well-known bearers.

Gideon

Gideon brandishes a fearless, muscular, and courageous impression. This robust name, which means "destroyer, feller of trees," suits an intrepid two-year-old who knocks down everything in his path as well as a brave Christian man who fights injustice. Though Gideon has doubts about his ability to carry out the Lord's assignment, he eventually defeats the evil Midianites. He is mentioned in the "Hall of Faith" as one of the men who "through faith conquered kingdoms . . . whose weakness was turned to strength" (Hebrews 11:33-34). Chosen by actor Mandy Patinkin for his son, Gideon is a vigorous alternative to the ultrapopular Jacob and Joshua.

Why We Named Our Son Gideon

Amy and I loved talking to our baby while he was still floating comfortably in his womb-world. One afternoon at work, the name Gideon came to my mind. I liked the strength and boldness it suggested; also not being a common name, the individuality of it appealed to me. Right away, I felt very strongly that this was the right name for our son, and (after having some time to think about it) Amy agreed. We told no one the name before his birth, so for several months it was known only to the three of us.

Gideon, our four-year-old, is so much more than my limited vision of him before his birth. He is strong of spirit, waking each day with an abandoned joy that is infectious, and approaching others with an open confidence that is the envy of his more timid father. Our prayer for him as he matures is that his character will grow to be equal in strength to his boldness and confidence.

—*Jonathan and Amy Stoner*

Isaac

Even in this age of test-tube babies and elaborate fertility treatments, the birth of a baby to a ninety-year-old woman would be a phenomenon. Isaac was the original miracle baby coming as he did in the sunset of Abraham and Sarah's life together. The couple called their long-awaited boy "laughter," which indicates they got a kick out of God's timing in fulfilling his promises to them. For couples who are anticipating the birth of their own miracle baby, Isaac would be an especially fitting name. Today Isaac seems to have a serious, scholarly patina, perhaps because the two most famous Isaacs are scientist Newton and violinist Stern. Ike is the more casual, gregarious nickname.

Isaiah

Isaiah is considered the greatest prophet in Scripture, so it's not surprising he was quoted fifty times in the New Testament. In his commissioning, Isaiah saw with photographic clarity a vivid vision of God seated on his throne and surrounded by seraphs. The first half of his book is filled with scorching blasts and pronouncements of doom. But in the second part, Isaiah softens up, filling the pages with the gladdening, unfolding promise of future blessings through his Messiah. Like his tome, Isaiah is both heavy-handed and tender. The weight and somberness of this boldly biblical name offsets its rather musical, euphonious sound. Apparently modern parents are liking this combination of style and substance: Isaiah is a rising star at number sixty. Former Detroit Piston Isaiah Thomas gives the name an athletic spin.

Jacob

Jacob means "held by the heel, supplanter," and Michael better watch out because this name superstar is nipping at his heels and about to supplant him as numero uno. Everybody loves Jacob, and as a result, the name is boiling-over hot. But what's not to like—apart from utter ubiquitousness? Handsome, manly Jacob has archaic roots, was revived about a century ago, cooled down, and is now the "it" boy. Though Jacob is thoroughly trendy, it doesn't scream "I was born in the nineties" quite so much as Brandon or Justin. After all, the patriarch Jacob was one of the most important people in the Old Testament. Highlights of his epic saga include conspiring with his mother, Rebekah, to wrench twin brother Esau's birthright away; working seven years to marry Rachel; wrestling with God; and fathering the twelve tribes of Israel. Jake is a high-energy nickname, though the cute short form "Cub" has also been heard. My two cents: Enough, already.

Jadon/Jared

Scouting for an alternative to Jacob? Look no further than Jadon and Jared. Because the top fifty seems to be sponsored by the letter *J* (Joshua, Justin, Jordan, Jason, and so on), it's time to dig deeply for some new names sporting this wildly popular consonant. These two Hebrew ID's have kept a low profile, although Jared is three spots away from cracking the top fifty. In Genesis 5, Jared ("the descendent"), who lived to a ripe old age of 962, is listed as a great-great-great grandson of Adam. Certainly a sturdy yet still interesting choice. Not even on the top one hundred, Jadon is even fresher: Fresh Prince Will Smith and actress Jada Pinkett Smith chose it for their baby son, as did Christian Slater. The biblical Jadon ("God has heard"), we are told in Nehemiah 3:7, lent some muscle to the rebuilding of the city walls of Jerusalem, specifically the Jeshanah Gate.

Jedidiah / Jeremiah

Welcome to the mountain-man page, where men live off the land, dine off of brook trout and bison, and sleep under the stars with their trusty yellow dogs by their sides. Can you imagine such bearded explorers as Jedidiah Strong Smith or Jeremiah Johnson as Bobs and Ricks? Neither can I. If your idea of camping is being dropped by helicopter into some remote region of the Yukon, these names are for you. Jeremiah was a bullfrog, according to Three Dog Night, but his name is a heap more interesting than most other *J* names in the pond. Meaning "God will raise up" and "the weeping prophet," Jeremiah was one of the major prophets in the Old Testament who authored a lengthy book of largely gloomy prophecies.

Jedidiah, also clad in tanned hides from head to toe, means "loved by God." Second Samuel 12:25 refers to Jedidiah as God's name for baby Solomon: "Because the LORD loved him, he sent word through Nathan the prophet to name him Jedidiah." Though mountain-man jobs went the way of the flintlock, modern-day Jeremiahs and Jedidiahs may aspire to something equally adventurous, like extreme sports or scaling Mount Everest. Both names would make rugged, innovative choices, but Jedidiah has a slight advantage: the "black gold, Texas tea" hillbilly nickname Jed.

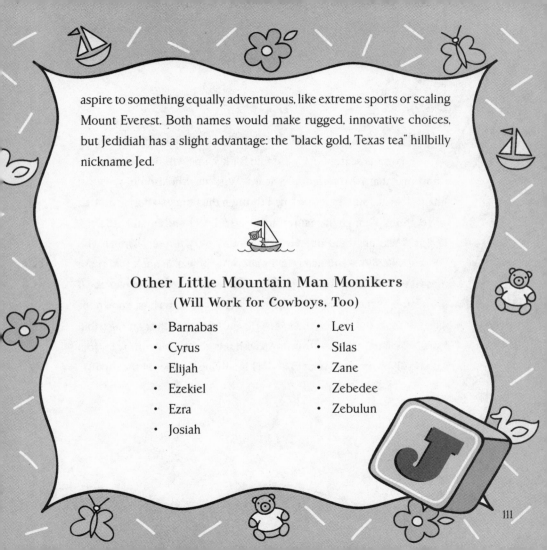

Other Little Mountain Man Monikers
(Will Work for Cowboys, Too)

- Barnabas
- Cyrus
- Elijah
- Ezekiel
- Ezra
- Josiah
- Levi
- Silas
- Zane
- Zebedee
- Zebulun

Joel

Currently Joel is out of the loop, which is a good thing for parents searching for a stable Bible name without a lot of flash, and one that isn't commonly heard. With its wholesome, sensitive image, Joel has suited boys-to-men through the fifties, sixties, seventies, and eighties. Though the name's image is laid-back and amiable, the biblical Joel was anything but. He was another fiery minor prophet who spoke explicitly and intensely in his short but powerful book. Joel's core message was a timeless call to repentance with the promise of grace if his hearers turned away from their sins. He is perhaps best known for using the dark illustration of a locust plague to warn of the coming tribulation. You won't raise any eyebrows with this choice, but opting for Joel would still be more original than the high-flying *J* names in the top five.

Beyond Tom, Dick, and Harry: Classics to Consider

Some boys' names are so durable, so safe, and so commonly heard, they hearken back to the days of ancient Rome, when only a dozen or so names were used for either sex. As Marcus and Brutus would have certainly shared their names with countless friends, relatives, and acquaintances, so today would Mark, Jim, and Mike each have to bring their own special qualities to their omnipresent tags. The enormous popularity of these names has resulted in their becoming so diluted they are virtually generic. But obviously, the general population is not deterred by overpopularity. Here is a list of stalwart names that may interest you:

- *Michael:* Good-hearted, manly, the superstar of baby names
- *Mark:* Sounds honest and true. Bonus: Only number sixty-six on the chart
- *John:* The number-one name for centuries and becoming fashionable again
- *Joseph:* Phenomenal biblical role model, plus Joe is as all-American as they get. Still number twelve
- *James:* Practical, compassionate James evokes the qualities he wrote about in his biblical book (number nineteen)

Jonah

Jonah, leading man in one of the Bible's most memorable stories, was God's prophet who ran from his divine assignment and was consequently regurgitated by a whale. While not the most teachable man in the Bible, Jonah did eventually fulfill his mission to preach a message of doom to one of the most powerful cities in the world. The name will always be associated with that dyspeptic whale, which could lead modern-day Jonahs to have an affinity for marine biology or a terror of Sea World. Because of this affiliation, Jonah has a rugged, outdoorsy image as bracing as the ocean air. An energetic alternative to the more prevalent, gentler Noah. Drawback: People will constantly be calling your child Noah anyway. Indeed, the two names appear to have similar linguistic roots because they share a meaning: "peace."

Why We Named Our Son Jonah

We both like to be outdoors. My husband lives to fish, and I have always been so drawn to the ocean. Jonah was a name we both liked right away because of its association with water and whales. Plus I once did an in-depth study of the book of Jonah and always thought the prophet was fascinating, stubborn, willful, yet in the end he did what was so hard to do. We are so glad we named our son Jonah! It seems to suit his strong will, and it is really fun to read "his" story in the Bible. People are always giving us whale stuff, and one of our relatives affectionately calls him "fish boy." My father-in-law used to say, portentously, "You know people can live up to or down to their name." In Jonah's case, we hope he appreciates his namesake's story and learns that doing the right thing the first time makes for a smoother and less fishy smelling life!

—*Lorilee and Doyle Craker*

Joshua

Joshua and his troops may have circulated Jericho seven times before it crashed, but I have a feeling we are going to go around Joshua many more times before it's done. For almost two decades Joshua has been ensconced on the top ten, and this blockbuster boys' name shows no signs of cooling off. Why? Moms like it, dads love it, teachers find it appealing—even other little kids can say "Josh." This Latin form of the Hebrew "Yeshua" ("Jesus" is the Greek translation) has an athletic muscle, a biblical backbone, and even a cowboyish kick for good measure. Joshua is the Michael of tomorrow. (It's even the Michael of today in some areas.) Thankfully this overheated name has a worthy biblical role model to support its behemoth popularity. Joshua, chosen by God to succeed Moses, led the Israelites through several enormous battles before leading them into the Promised Land.

Josiah

If you love Joshua's rhythm and western flair, Josiah ("God supports") could be your saving grace from generic baby naming. Josiah still sounds fresh and new, because, low and behold, it hasn't even cracked the top one hundred yet. And it gets even better: Josiah was an outstanding role model in Scripture. The last of the good kings of Judah, Josiah assumed the throne at the age of eight, and his rule of thirty-one years was marked by renewal and revival. "Neither before nor after Josiah was there a king like him who turned to the LORD as he did—with all his heart and with all his soul and with all his strength" (2 Kings 23:25). With a great contemporary sound and a pedigree like that, the only wonder is that Josiah hasn't caught on in a huge way. It can be abbreviated to Joe (but don't you dare!), Joss, or even Josey (too girlie? Think Clint Eastwood in *The Outlaw Josey Wales*).

If You Like Michael, You'll Love Micah

Baby-namers tend to be attracted to the same sound combinations or qualities in the names that catch their fancy. Take the couple who named their sons Brady, Brandon, and Bradley, for instance. No surprises there. Others are attracted to place names, ethnic names, classic names, or eccentric, arty names. Here are the top ten boys' names and a few more interesting, fresher options. If you are attracted to the bestseller, hopefully you will also appreciate its lesser-known alternative:

1. *Michael:* Ethan, Josiah, Micah
2. *Jacob:* Abram, Jadon, Jared
3. *Matthew:* Nathanael, Luke, Seth
4. *Joshua:* Jeremiah, Jonah, Josiah
5. *Christopher:* Benjamin, Nathanael, Peter
6. *Nicholas:* Adam, Barnabas, Isaac, Micah
7. *Brandon:* Aaron, Adam, Ethan, Jadon
8. *Tyler:* Jadon, Jared, Tabor
9. *Andrew:* Aaron, Abram, Adam, Anders
10. *Austin:* Ethan, Kenan, Jotham

Jotham

Jotham (rhymes with Gotham or can be pronounced JOH-thum) would make an exceptionally imaginative, futuristic choice. This hybrid of Joshua and Ethan has a very "now" sound that should appeal to independent thinkers. Meaning "God is perfect," Jotham can hardly be found in baby-name books, never mind on the playground, so the way is clear for you to road test it on your street. Happily the biblical guy has an actual story, not just a passing reference. Jotham was a young, godly king of Judah who Scripture says "grew powerful because he walked steadfastly before the LORD his God" (2 Chronicles 27:6). King Jotham's reign was short (sixteen years) but sweet: He initiated a major new infrastructure in Judah and conquered the Ammonites in a decisive victory. Unlike his father, Uzziah, Jotham never caved in to pride but stayed humbly committed to God's ways until his death. Yes, Joth is sort of Josh with a lisp—everyone will soon get used to it!

Brother Combos

- *Corned-Beef-and-Cabbage Cubs:* Kenan, Malachi
- *Trendy Tots:* Jake, Josh, Nick, Zach
- *Bible Basics Boys:* Andrew, Daniel, David, Joel, Matthew, Paul, Peter, Philip, Stephen, Thomas, Timothy
- *L'il Cowpokes Posse:* Cyrus, Josiah, Levi, Luke, Zach, Zane, Zeb, Zeke
- *Mini-Mountain-Man Mob (mix and match with posse):* Amos, Bartholomew, Elijah, Jedidiah, Jeremiah, Silas
- *One Singular Sensation Set:* Asher, Barnabas, Gideon, Jotham, Kenan, Malachi, Philemon, Silas, Tabor, Zebedee
- *Cirque de Quirk (works with the singular sensation names, too):* Boaz, Bartholomew, Cyrus, Ezekiel, Felix, Linus, Meshach, Moses, Rufus
- *Trailblazer Tribe:* Abram, Eli, Ezra, Gideon, Isaiah, Jadon, Jonah, Kenan, Levi, Malachi, Reuben, Zane
- *Chart-Climbing Club:* Benjamin, Caleb, Elijah, Gabriel, Isaac, Josiah, Micah, Nathanael
- *Handsome Classics Clan:* Aaron, Adam, Ethan, Luke, Nathan, Peter, Samuel, Zachary

Kenan

Kenan is definitely a buzz name, with several signs pointing to its future popularity. First of all it sounds Irish, a benefit that launched Aidan, Keiran, and the hot Keagan into use among style-setters. This cheerful Irish kick isn't a coincidence: Three saints from the Emerald Isle wore this high-energy name. Also it's being heard on TV via Nickelodeon's bouncing-off-the-ceiling kids' show *Kenan and Kel*. Finally the letter *K* should see some heat with the inevitable cool down of molten neighbor *J*. Kenan (Gaelic: "ancient"; Hebrew: "to acquire or possess") was listed in Genesis 5:14 as one of Adam's extremely hardy descendants, who died when he was 910.

Popular African-American Boys' Names from the Bible

- Amos*
- Andrew*
- Benjamin*
- Clement
- Cornelius
- Darius*
- Demetrius
- Isaiah*
- Jared*
- Jason
- Kenan*
- Meshach*
- Michael
- Noah*
- Omar
- Rufus*
- Samuel*
- Simeon

*Profiles found elsewhere in *"A" Is for Adam*

Levi

Levi strongly suggests a dude rancher who likes his coffee just this side of mud. Yep, Levi's a quintessential cowboy name redolent of the old west and all the action and adventure that era rustles up. Of course the guy who single-handedly imbued this name with such a hearty, manly rep was the Jewish jeans entrepreneur Levi Strauss. *The Baby Name Survey Book* backs me up on this one: "Like the jeans that bear this name, Levi is regarded as a rugged, down-to-earth, and masculine cowboy or westerner." Still well underused (unless it has already caught on in your church or neighborhood), Levi ("devotion") is a worthy peer of Jonah, Josiah, and Micah—"now"-sounding biblical names that still haven't hit the top one hundred. The third of Jacob's sons, Levi begot descendants who became the priestly order of Levites. Lee or Lev suffice as variations.

Luke

For some reason, the one-syllable idea has never really caught on with boys' names like it has with girls'. Luke is an exception, sharing the straightforward, sporty appeal of Jack or Hank. At number sixty, Goldilocks would say this name is neither too hot nor too cold—it's just right. Luke has an innate warmth, a friendly, amiable nature that is no doubt influenced by the biblical apostle of the same name. In Luke (he also penned Acts), the kind doctor highlighted Jesus' compassion, especially for women. As the patron saint of doctors, Luke has been bestowed on countless hospitals. Pop culture influences include Luke Skywalker as the good guy and Luke Duke as the good ol' boy. Luc, as in hockey star Luc Robitaille, is a novel idea if you have a French connection.

Why We Named Our Son Luke

We named our first son Luke after the author of the gospel and the book of Acts. Luke was a physician, historian, and dedicated coworker with the apostle Paul. But more, he was an educated man who came to know, love, and serve Jesus Christ. After Christ's ascension he carefully researched and gathered the stories of Jesus' ministry and compiled them into a compelling history.

When our son was born, I was in the middle of law school and surrounded by the attitude that faith in Christ is unintelligent. To counterbalance this philosophy, we wanted him to carry with him a reminder that many of the strongest and most educated people in history have been deeply committed followers of Christ. We hope the name blesses Luke with the confidence that faith in Christ is reasonable, historical, and true.

—Kyle and Sandy Netterfield

Malachi

Irish parents take note: Instead of honoring your child's ethnic roots with an Emerald Isle ID such as Liam or Connor, why not also express your faith by picking the winning Malachi? This upbeat, strong-sounding name has a heroic history in Ireland, where the original Malachi was a king who defeated Norse invaders. If you dare to be extremely, genuinely Irish, there is the original mouthful "Maolmhaodhog." Also an Irish connection: Malachi is the name of the lead character in James Joyce's *Ulysses*. In the Old Testament, Malachi was the last of the twelve minor prophets who urged the Jews to turn from their unfaithfulness and restore their relationship with God. His vivid word pictures—"the sun of righteousness will rise with healing in its wings" (Malachi 4:2)—were the hallmark of his preaching style. The name boasts a fun, friendly duo of nicknames: Mac and Mal.

Matthew

Matthew, says Joal Ryan, is a "monster pocket T" as trend-resistant and fashion-safe as pairing jeans with a white T-shirt. On the charts for three decades, Matthew draws raves for its casual, laid-back personality and strong, decent image. From the Hebrew Mattathiah, Matthew ("gift of God") became one of Jesus' disciples. Formerly a despised Jewish tax collector, Matthew responded immediately to Jesus' call to leave his lucrative work and follow him. Later the disciple would put his accounting skills to work when he wrote his detailed gospel. This alias is handsome and appealing, but obviously there is no shortage of Matthews (Gen X actors Bodine, Broderick, Perry, Damon, and McConaughey currently display this fact). Matthias, offbeat and interesting, belonged to the disciple chosen to replace Judas Iscariot. Or if you have a hint of Latin lineage (and even if you don't), Mateo boasts a rousing, global beat.

Meshach

Meshach might be too wild for some families, but it isn't unheard-of in the same way as flame-resistant brethren Shadrach and Abednego. In fact this lively, personable name is well used among African-American families including actor Meshach Taylor's. The biblical bearer, along with his aforementioned friends, would be a worthy and valorous role model for any boy who will thrill to the exciting details of his namesake's story. Shadrach, Meshach, and Abednego defied King Nebuchadnezzar's orders to fall down and worship the image of gold. Instead the brave lads risked the fiery furnace and certain death rather than capitulate. Of course they were miraculously saved without a hair on their heads being singed (Daniel 3). With loads of personality and a fresh, vibrant sound, Meshach should be a viable choice for parents on the lookout for daring, bright, and imaginative names.

The Top Fifty Boys Names

1. Michael	18. Anthony	35. Hunter
2. Jacob*	19. James	36. Cameron
3. Matthew*	20. Justin	37. Aaron*
4. Joshua*	21. Jonathan	38. Ethan*
5. Christopher	22. Alexander	39. Eric
6. Nicholas*	23. Kyle	40. Jason
7. Brandon	24. Robert	41. Brian
8. Tyler	25. Christian	42. Caleb*
9. Andrew*	26. Dylan	43. Cody
10. Austin	27. Jordan*	44. Logan
11. Daniel*	28. Samuel*	45. Luis
12. Joseph	29. Jose	46. Adam*
13. William	30. Kevin	47. Steven*
14. Zachary*	31. Noah*	48. Connor
15. John	32. Benjamin*	49. Timothy*
16. David*	33. Thomas*	50. Charles
17. Ryan	34. Nathan*	

*Profiles found elsewhere in "A" Is for Adam

Micah

Micah pulls off a neat trick: It has all the handsomeness and strength of huge next-door-neighbor Michael (at number one for decades on end) but without being anywhere near the trendy zone. In fact this Hebrew name, meaning "who is like God," hasn't even touched the top one hundred (it's just a matter of time). The best known of the biblical Micahs was the prophet and author whose book is threaded with lovely Hebrew poetry amidst his main message: a trouncing of the ruling classes and their wicked ways. Many Christians hold as their favorite Bible verse Micah 6:8, which sets forth the standard required by God of his people "to act justly and to love mercy and to walk humbly with your God." As for the nickname Mike, haven't we all been there oh, about seven million times? Micah sounds fantastic the way it is.

Why We Named Our Son Micah

Today marks one year of life with our precious son. This birthday reflection brings the rare opportunity to remember the days leading up to his birth. It seems as if we know better today, in hindsight, why we chose the name and why it's perfect for our son. Micah is indicative of strength in humility. A merciful name. What we could never have known was that Micah's birth would reveal a deadly disease in his mother that would otherwise never have been found. This was God's gift of new life and extended life. Our prayer for our son is that his life will emulate the words written in Micah 6:8. God is using Micah's birth to mold our whole family into his image.

—*Paulo and Lisa Freire*

Moses

It seems like just yesterday that Moses would be considered way too much for a little tyke to bear. Under the Cecil B. De Mille regime—when the name was burdened with images of Charleton Heston's snowy beard and epic hairdo—Moses sounded altogether too ponderous. Today Moe's got a new M.O.: The amazing "Prince of Egypt." The animated film definitely injected some much needed youthfulness to the name, making it a plausible if not completely accessible choice. Satran and Rosenkratz concur: "A definite candidate for rejuvenation." Mia Farrow was, as usual, way ahead of the times when she named her adopted son Moses, and basketball legend Moses Malone gave the name some hoop appeal. In Exodus, Moses' tale unfolds from prince to shepherd to leader, prophet, lawgiver, and most important, friend of God. Bonus: As a nickname, Moe is uncommonly cool.

Nathan

At number thirty-four, it would seem that Nathan still has plenty of mileage left, but in many pockets this Hebrew name is commonly used. This is true especially in church nurseries where there are sure to be two or three Nathans running around. Meaning "God has given," Nathan is intellectual, old-fashioned, upwardly mobile—all the qualities parents search for without even knowing it. In *The Baby Name Survey Book*, Nathan was described as being "either a quiet, capable, and trustworthy man or a sneaky gangster who wears a suit like Nathan Detroit from the musical *Guys and Dolls*." The biblical Nathan, a prophet, was a truly courageous man who wasn't afraid to confront the mighty King David about his secret sins. The result was David's repenting and experiencing God's grace anew (2 Samuel 12). (By the way, David named one of his sons by Bathsheba, Nathan.) Nate is a winning short form.

Nathanael

If you love Nathan but want something a little less used, have we got a bargain for you! Nathanael emanates all the kindness, smarts, and decency of Nathan, but at a good 50 percent less popular. At number fifty-nine, Nathanael is on the rise but likely won't reach the saturation level anytime soon. Again *The Baby Name Survey Book* provides insights into mass opinion: "Nathanael has two very different images, an outgoing, lighthearted mischief-maker, or a quiet, conservative, dignified man—a minister perhaps." The New Testament Nathanael (spelled "Nathanel" or "Nathaneel" in some translations) was a disciple of Christ, a "true Israelite" or one who accepts Jesus by faith (John 1:47-50), and one of those privileged to speak with Jesus after his resurrection (John 21:1-14). A lesser-known Nathanael (spelled "Nathanel" or "Nathaneel" in some translations) was King David's brother (1 Chronicles 2:14). Infusing literary essence is Nathaniel Hawthorne, not to mention the character in Dickens's *The Pickwick Papers*, while crooner Nat King Cole adds an "unforgettable" musical flair.

Nicholas

Nicholas is just a flat-out gorgeous name, one that conveys character, nobility, charm and sweetness all in one fell swoop. The most famous Nicholas is the jolly old Christmas icon, the patron saint of children whose Americanized name is Santa Claus. This connection gives Nicholas lots of warm fuzzies while the doomed Czar Nicholas of Russia imbues this name with a dramatic, imperial bearing. In Acts 6:5, Nicolas is named as one of the seven assistants to the disciples. Naturally these shining attributes have not gone unnoticed by parents who have catapulted Nicholas to number six on the top-ten list. I agree heartily with Joal Ryan who suggests Nicholas may have reached its "critical mass." As stunning as it is, you can stick a fork in it—Nicholas is done. For creative spins on the theme, why not try a variation from your own ethnic background? Nicolaas (Dutch); Nikolaus (German); Niccolo (Italian); Nikolai (Russian).

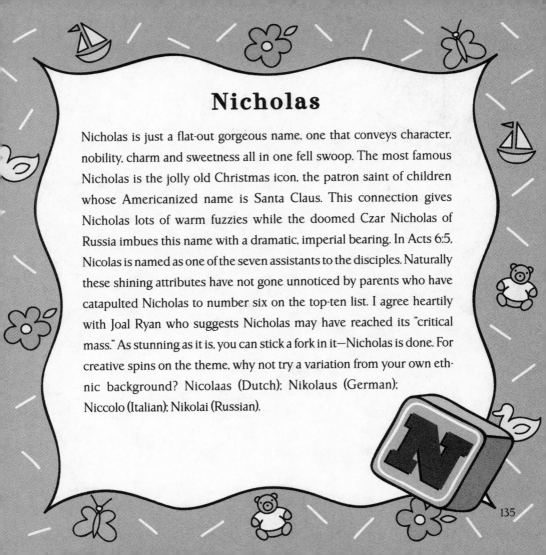

Noah

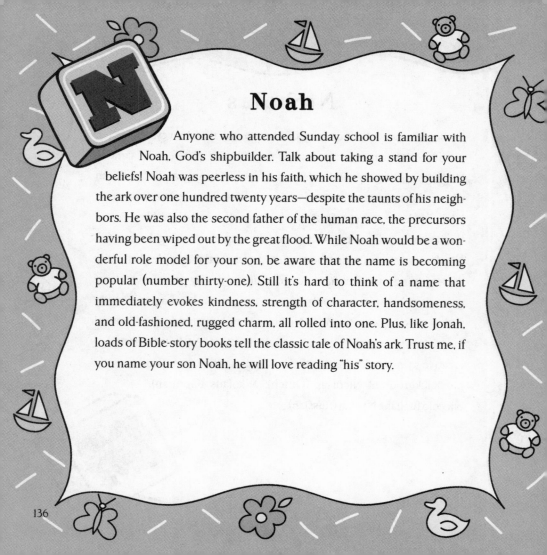

Anyone who attended Sunday school is familiar with Noah, God's shipbuilder. Talk about taking a stand for your beliefs! Noah was peerless in his faith, which he showed by building the ark over one hundred twenty years—despite the taunts of his neighbors. He was also the second father of the human race, the precursors having been wiped out by the great flood. While Noah would be a wonderful role model for your son, be aware that the name is becoming popular (number thirty-one). Still it's hard to think of a name that immediately evokes kindness, strength of character, handsomeness, and old-fashioned, rugged charm, all rolled into one. Plus, like Jonah, loads of Bible-story books tell the classic tale of Noah's ark. Trust me, if you name your son Noah, he will love reading "his" story.

Why We Named Our Son Noah

As two people who work in and with the church for a living, we tend to be passionate about things biblical. Thus it seemed the natural choice to look to the Bible when naming our children. For our second child we chose the name Noah (our first is Benjamin). In our little Noah, we pray for the same love and respect for creation that is so completely a part of my husband, and so completely a part of what the biblical Noah was about. We pray that he has that same overwhelming trust in the Lord and that deep, all-consuming desire to do God's will no matter what the cost. We pray that he will always be certain and steadfast in the covenants God has made with him. When we gave Noah his name while he was still in the womb, we had no idea what he might be like. Therefore I find it so amazing that each day he grows more and more into his name, affirming the way God's spirit works in our lives!

—Melissa and Howard Bonser

Paul

Other than Jesus, the apostle Paul had more influence in Christianity than any other person. A fierce persecutor of Christians before his conversion, Paul never lost his fiery dedication, boldness, and strong personality. After his shocking encounter with God on the road to Damascus, he applied his formidable strengths to spreading the gospel. The greatest missionary, theologian, and soul-winner in church history, Paul wrote thirteen of the New Testament books. Given the name Saul at birth, the apostle took the name Paul, meaning "small, little," after his decision to depend on God's power. Despite this potent history, Paul sounds a bit tired and dated at this point, like an avocado-green sofa from 1972. But what goes around comes around—even avocado green—so Paul could possibly stage a comeback. Three cool ethnic spins: Paulo (Portuguese); Pablo (Spanish); Pavel (Russian).

Peter

His given name was Simon bar Jonah, but the apostle Peter was renamed by Christ—an event that signified that the brash, emotive disciple would be the capstone of Jesus' beloved church: "And I tell you that you are Peter, and on this rock I will build my church, and the gates of Hades will not overcome it" (Matthew 16:18). As the first great leader of the Christian church and one of the "inner three" group of Jesus' closest friends, Peter is one of the most richly spiritual names in history. Quaintly old-fashioned, gentle, and bold all at once, Peter would be a strong choice for parents searching for a classic biblical name that isn't commonly heard, at least not in recent years. Peter is one of the few familiar Bible names that isn't on the top one hundred.

Philemon

The book of Philemon is one of shortest in Scripture, only twenty-five verses in length. Written by Paul to his friend the affluent Colossian Philemon, the letter is a brilliant template of what it means to confront someone in Christian love. Paul begins by pointing out Philemon's stellar qualities of faith, love, and encouragement; then he tactfully appeals to the wealthy landowner to accept his runaway slave, Onesimus, back as a Christian brother. Daredevil baby-namers may warm to Philemon's funky, hip-sounding form, but obviously this Greek name meaning "beloved, kiss" won't float most people's boats. Phi is the academic sounding short form, and Lee might work too. Maybe.

Philip

Though Philip has an illustrious history as a name, not to mention a remarkable biblical role model, the Greek alias ("lover of horses") still suffers from a slight image problem. While debonair and brainy on one hand, Philip also suggests a bit of conceit and pampering. You may want to work around the negatives, however, when you focus on Philip's many great qualities, including his New Testament namesakes. The first and lesser-known Philip was an apostle who lead Nathanael to Christ. The second was also a tireless evangelist. When Philip the deacon shared Christ with the Ethiopian official (whose job would be the equivalent of Alan Greenspan's today), he was converted and baptized immediately. (Many believe this divinely appointed meeting was the seed that spread the gospel in Africa.) Nicknames include Phil (yawn), Flip (peppy!), Phillie (works for a sandwich, too). Pip is precious, but just add "squeak" and you've got problems on the playground.

Reuben

Reuben, one of the most interesting, underused names from the Bible, is sounding more like a retro-cool baby name and less like someone's Jewish grandpa all the time. Attribute this change in perception to the character Reuben in the wildly popular musical *Joseph and the Amazing Technicolor Dreamcoat*, or simply to tastes that are widening in search of Bible names beyond Jacob and Joshua. As Jacob and Leah's firstborn son, Reuben talked his brothers out of actually killing Joseph, but then didn't do much more to protect him (Genesis 37:21-22). Later he made amends, sort of, when he offered his own sons as a guarantee that Benjamin would be safe in Egypt (Genesis 42:37). Yes, Reuben has a definite deli flavor, but it also carries an upbeat, "C'mon Get Happy" vibe thanks to the character on *The Partridge Family*, manager Reuben Kincaid. With roguish Rube as a nickname, Reuben should go places in the next decade.

Why We Named Our Son Reuben

My wife, Dawn, and I wanted a name that was meaningful, distinctive, and pleasant-sounding, plus we had a preference for biblical names. Our early list of male names included Reuben (Hebrew for "see, a son"), but we couldn't fully agree on a single name for either gender.

Despite our strong preference for a natural birth, after thirty hours of labor we ended up having the baby via C-section. As the doctor pulled the baby from Dawn's womb, he said, "It's a boy!" and I could clearly see that indeed it was. Based partly on my experience of his birth ("See, a son!"), we named our son Reuben, after Jacob's firstborn son in the Bible. We felt it would be uncommon enough to distinguish him from other boys and men throughout his life, and we liked the way "Reuben" rolled off the tongue and landed on the ear with a pleasing ring.

—*Joel and Dawn Niewenhuis*

Latino Bible Names for Boys

- Jacob: Jacobo
- John: Juan
- Joshua: Josué
- Luke: Lucas
- Mark: Marcos
- Matthew: Mateo
- Michael: Miguel

- Moses: Moisès
- Peter: Pedro
- Philip: Felipe
- Raphael: Raphael
- Samuel: Samuel
- Steven: Esteban
- Zechariah: Zacarias

Rufus

Rufus was among the close group of friends mentioned in Paul's personal greetings to the Romans. This friend and church member was "chosen in the Lord," so the apostle notes in Romans 16:13. An expansive, quirky tag, Rufus isn't for everyone, but it may just be the ticket for iconoclast baby-namers who can't wait for the day when solar-powered cars are a reality. *The Baby Name Survey Book* says, "People think of Rufus as temperamental grouch who is a wild and crazy oddball." I personally think the name is a lot friendlier. Meaning "redhead," Rufus conjures up a guy with a wild, curly carrot top, an irresistible smile, and a tie-dyed shirt, handing out antiwar pamphlets with a smile. FYI: Rufus has a strong presence on the African-American charts. There was also a Revolutionary War general by the name of Rufus Putnam.

Samuel

Samuel ("hand of God"), one of the most stylish names of the last two decades, brings up highly positive associations of goodness, character, and an earthy, homey sense of humor. The biblical Samuel was a pivotal Old Testament figure who is considered the greatest judge, an effective leader who bridged the gap between the judges and Israel's kings. Most Bible characters are hard to picture as children, but Samuel's story unfolds from the time before he was born when his mother Hannah promised him to God's service in the temple (1 Samuel 1:28). His life teaches that serving God is for people of all ages, not just adults. Samuel shares the lovable nickname Sam with Samson, but that's about all the two had in common. While Samson might be more creative at this point, his penchant for wild women and worldliness rules him out as a role model. In this case, stick with the classic.

Seth

Seth is a clean, woodsy name that wears a flannel shirt and a pair of cowboy boots (could that image spring from the many western flicks with sensitive dudes named Seth?). One would expect a guy named Seth to be kind, laid-back, and hardworking. Joal Ryan says, "Seth easily travels in the same circles as sensitive, cute boys Justin and Joshua." At first glance, Seth's role in Scripture is slight: He was Adam and Eve's third son, born after his brother Cain killed his brother Abel. A closer look reveals that Seth was the start of a new beginning for humans, the child who would take Abel's place as a leader in the line of God's devoted people. Seth is mentioned in Christ's lineage after Adam (Luke 3:38). Well underused at number eighty-nine, Seth is also happily impossible to shorten.

Silas

If Silas were a food, it would definitely be something as relaxed and homespun as fried chicken, hush puppies, and collard greens. According to Rosenkratz and Satran, earthy Silas "has a funky feel appealing to parents who long to return to the soil." Fittingly this Greek name, a short form of Silouanus, means "of the trees" or "from the forest." In Acts 15:26-27, Silas is named as one of the "men who have risked their lives for the name of our Lord Jesus Christ." Indeed the brave missionary endured beatings, prison, an earthquake, and numerous narrow escapes in his quest to carry the gospel to the ends of the earth. The coauthor of 1 Peter, Silas was the first bishop of Corinth according to legend. Rarely heard, Silas would be a warm, unusual, and inventive choice.

Simon

Despite its suave British accents, erudite Simon is really a very direct, accessible, and homey kind of name. Well used in England, Simon has been borne by numerous British heroes, including roguish spy Simon Templar in the TV and movie productions of *The Saint*. Greek for "Shimon," Simon means "one who hears." There were many Simons mentioned in Scripture, including Simon of Cyrene who carried Jesus' cross to Calvary, Simon Peter, and Simon the Zealot, one of the twelve who may have been involved in a radical political party working to oust Romans from Jerusalem (Matthew 10:4). Nowhere near trendy, Simon would be a fresh, fashionable, and fun option for parents seeking something just a tad offbeat. Simeon, the Anglicized version, was the name of the old priest who blessed the infant Jesus at the temple (Luke 2:25-35).

Stephen

Stephen is like John, David, Mark, and James. None of them are particularly overused at the moment, but in the past they have been high on the charts, resulting in a surplus of those names. Stephen is still quite dignified though, and handsome to boot, if not original. With the unusual meaning "crown," Stephen has been one of the most popular Christian names throughout history. The biblical bearer is one of Scripture's most valorous figures who boldly pronounced his faith before the Sanhedrin, risking his life. Indeed while being stoned to death, Stephen prayed for his killers' forgiveness. Bottom line: Great role model, tired name. You could get infinitely more mileage out of Stephen at this point by using an ethnic version: Stefan (German, Swedish, Slavic); Stefano (Italian); Esteban (Spanish); Stavros (Greek).

Don't Say You Haven't Been Warned
Highly Unadvisable Boys' Names

- Apollos *(major narcissism ahead)*
- Beno *(sounds like a gas remedy)*
- Crispus *(crispy on the outside, flaky on the inside)*
- Darkon *(shades of "Luke, I am your father")*
- Blastus *(too blasted angry)*
- Ebenezer *(too sneezy and scroogy)*
- Gad *(sounds like "God" with a wicked Wisconsin accent)*
- Haggai *(avoid the prefix "Hag" at all costs)*
- Harim *(you don't want your kid to get any funny ideas when he starts dating)*
- Ichabod *(the whole headless horseman thing killed this one)*
- Jaazaniah *(way too hard to pronounce)*
- Jehoshaphat *(a little jumpy, don't you think?)*
- Lazarus *(too much pressure)*
- Ram *(when he's two he's going to be enough like a bull in a china shop)*

Tabor

Aha! A new discovery in baby names so fresh, so "now," so cool, people will think you invented it to ride the Tanner, Tyler, Taylor, Travis bandwagon. But the best part is you didn't make it up: Tabor is a place name in the Bible, a mountain near the Sea of Galilee where Deborah's ten thousand warriors charged and defeated Sisera's army (Judges 4). With victorious, mighty connotations like that, Tabor has loads of vitality and confidence. The beauty of this name is even though you will be blazing a new trail with it, Tabor still fits in amazingly well with the trendy sounds of today. If you are after one singular sensation, grab this one.

Thomas

Thomas has always gotten a bum rap for doubting, but actually he was a man of great faith. When it became apparent that Jesus was in grave danger, Thomas alone voiced his loyalty: "Let us also go, that we may die with him" (John 11:16). The apostle's questions were the product of a mind that searched honestly and diligently for the truth. The moment he examined Jesus' hands and side after his resurrection, Thomas believed. As a name, Thomas ("twin") is pure classic, a gentlemanly, intelligent alias that implies a thinking person. At number thirty-three, Thomas has risen above generic pals Dick and Harry with some serious staying power (although Harry's looking hot in England). Tommy works the cute angle—not to mention the fashion tack—but most modern parents will prefer Thomas in its fullest form.

Timothy

Timothy, like Peter and Philip, is a classic biblical name that has somehow avoided the overcooked status of the Davids and the Michaels, and the faddishness of Joshua and Jacob. In Scripture the young missionary and pastor was a disciple and companion of Paul's. The apostle also addressed two epistles to him. Meaning "honored of God," Timothy is a naurally beautiful name with inherent sweetness and goodness. For the PB&J crowd, Timmy is an option, but then you would be obliged to call your dog Lassie. Timothy also has a boyish feeling that works well for a little guy.

Bible Baby Names from the Great Books

Book	Author	Names
Anna Karenina	Leo Tolstoy	Anna
As You Like It	Shakespeare	Adam, Phoebe
The Castle	Franz Kafka	Barnabas
Catcher in the Rye	J. D. Salinger	Phoebe
Daphnis and Chloe	Longus	Chloe
David Copperfield	Charles Dickens	Uriah
Fathers and Sons	Ivan Turgenev	Nikolai
The Great Gatsby	F. Scott Fitzgerald	Jordan
Moby Dick	Herman Melville	Ahab, Ishmael
1984	George Orwell	Julia
Paradise Lost	John Milton	Adam, Gabriel, Raphael
The Pioneers	James Fenimore Cooper	Jotham
Pride and Prejudice	Jane Austen	Elizabeth, Lydia
Silas Marner	George Eliot	Silas
Sons and Lovers	D. H. Lawrence	Miriam
The Tempest	Shakespeare	Ariel
To the Lighthouse	Virginia Woolf	Lily
Ulysses	James Joyce	Malachi
Utopia	Thomas More	Thomas
Vanity Fair	Thackeray	Jemimah

Zachary / Zechariah

Rugged and righteous, tough yet tender, Zachary has all the components parents are looking for in a boy's name. No wonder it is firmly entrenched on the top fifteen. Dads-to-be seem especially enthused about Zachary's stalwart image. The one thing that prevents this short form of Zechariah from being perfect is its widespread usage. At this point you wouldn't be plowing any new ground with Zachary. But if it is the name of your dreams, take heart: Like Michael, Zachary's classic qualities save it from utter faddishness, but unlike Mike, the nickname Zach still has some zip. FYI: Zachary Taylor was the twelfth U.S. president. Zechariah, Zachary's parent company so to speak, was a prophet who authored an Old Testament book and, in the New Testament, was the father of John the Baptist.

Why We Named Our Son Zachary

"We don't have a boy's name yet," was our oft-repeated refrain during my entire pregnancy. A girl's name had come quickly and beautifully: Morgan. But a boy's name was something to be reckoned with. It had to be strong and manly, nothing girly in this household. There could be no names affiliated with football, basketball, or baseball players whom we disliked, or those who had bad reputations. No old boyfriends of mine or names with weird spellings or anything too unusual, and on and on. And then one day it happened. As I skimmed the last pages of a baby-name book, laughing at the improbable thought of having a child with a *Z* name—it hit me. Zachary. "Zachary Daniel!" I exclaimed. "Not bad," said Dan (so much for excited responses). After much deliberation it was declared "the one," but only on a trial basis. When our baby was delivered a surprising six weeks early, however, Zachary quickly became his name. That tiny baby—our son—had the perfect name for him.

—*Twila and Dan Bennett*

Golden Oldies: Charts from the Days of Your Great-Grandpa, Your Grandpa, Your Dad, and You

1900	1925	1950	1970
1. John	1. John	1. John	1. Michael
2. William	2. William	2. James	2. David
3. James	3. James	3. Robert	3. John
4. George	4. Robert	4. William	4. James
5. Charles	5. Charles	5. Michael	5. Robert
6. Joseph	6. Joseph	6. David	6. Christopher
7. Frank	7. George	7. Richard	7. William
8. Henry	8. Edward	8. Thomas	8. Mark
9. Robert	9. Frank	9. Charles	9. Richard
10. Harry	10. Thomas	10. Ronald	10. Brian

Zane

Heroic Zane is a sharp, urban cowboy name with a wonderfully craggy, unvarnished image as rugged as a wrangler from one of Zane Grey's western novels. All *Z* names have extra energy, but Zane may have even more of the good stuff packed into one high voltage syllable. Joal Ryan calls Zane "Hank with a *Z*." She says this name "is a pick to click. Zane works on a number of levels. It sounds handsome, looks dignified, and projects decency." Zane has an obscure reference in the Bible as the name of a plant mentioned in 2 Chronicles 16:14, but only some translations have kept it. Meanings range from "nourished" to "grace of God," but no matter what it means, Zane's got the goods to propel itself into the top one hundred.

Zebulun, Zebedee & Zebadiah

Zach is boiling over; Zane and Zeke are warming up. Turn on the back burner: Zeb is ready to cook. This means the formal versions of Zeb should be considered even if they are only used in a declarative sentence ("Zebulun Norman Snodgrass—if I've told you once, I've told you a thousand times . . .") or to grace the front cover of his first book. Zebadiah ("gift of the Lord") was the moniker of the temple gatekeeper (1 Chronicles 26:2) and one of King David's officers (1 Chronicles 27:7). Zebulun ("honored, exalted"), chosen by novelist Bret Lott *(Jewel)* for his son, was Jacob's boy who later fathered one of the twelve tribes. Zebedee (Zebedy is another spelling), as a short form of Zebadiah, shares the meaning "gift of the Lord." He was noted in Scripture as being the head of a fishing family, the father of disciples James and John (Mark 1:19-20). All three sparkle with the *Z* zing and are grounded by biblical antecedents and mountain-man/Wild West imagery.